ROYAL
Fashion
&
Beauty
SECRETS

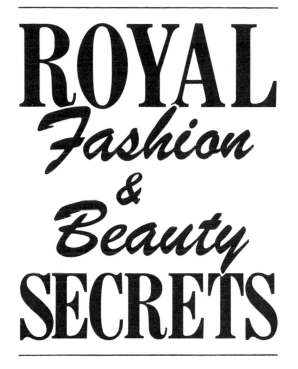

ROYAL
Fashion
& Beauty
SECRETS

**An Intimate Look at How
Princess Diana Achieves Her Radiance,
Style, and Grace—Revealed
for Women Everywhere**

Ann Chubb

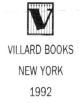

VILLARD BOOKS

NEW YORK

1992

Originally published in Great Britain in 1992 by Vermilion
an imprint of Ebury Press
Random House UK Ltd
Random House
20 Vauxhall Bridge Road
London SW1V 2SA

ISBN 0 679 74448 7

LC 92-50545

Editor: Alison Wormleighton
Design: Jerry Goldie
Illustrator: Tony Hannaford

Typeset by Textype Typesetters, Cambridge

Printed and bound in Italy by New Interlitho S.p.a.

First American Edition

Contents

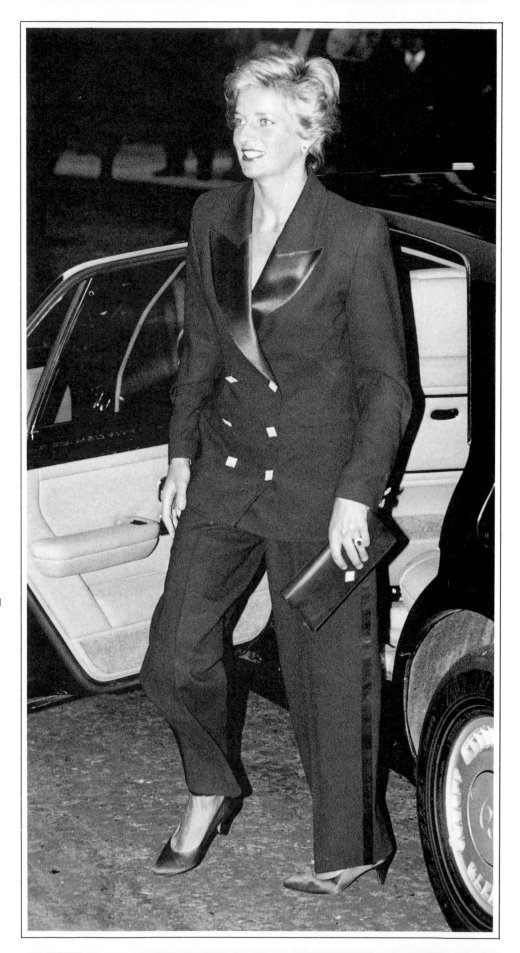

Picture of a modern princess: the fashionable Princess of Wales steps out for a night on the town in the way she loves best to dress, whether it's a private or a public engagement. No tiara, no grand jewels and no elaborate ballgown – instead a contemporary cropped haircut and a sophisticated smoking suit with sleek, mannish lines.

Introduction

This is a modern-day fairy tale. It is the story of a pretty but relatively ordinary English rose who has been transformed, Cinderella-style, into a radiant princess.

Little more than a decade ago, Lady Diana Spencer was a plump, shy teenager. Today, as Princess of Wales and the future Queen of England, she is the world's favourite cover girl, with a model figure and couture wardrobe to match.

The story of just how this young woman has transformed herself into the most photographed beauty in the world is a fascinating one. It provides a revealing insight into the self-discipline and sheer will-power, coupled with the desire for self-improvement, that lay behind her dramatic metamorphosis.

The Princess of Wales has spared no time, trouble or money to find the very best experts in each field, be it hairdressing or holistic cures, fashion or fitness.

She has done it, not for vanity, but because her clothes, her looks, her figure and, above all, her health are very much part of the whole business of being a royal personage. And business it is. In private life, Princess Diana often wears jeans and sweatshirts just like any other young mother, but she knows full well that every time she steps outside her front door the lenses of the world's press will be focused on her and she must do them justice.

In fact, the slim Princess exercises as much for energy as for weight control. Furthermore, she has learned by trial and error to eliminate what doesn't suit her, and has simplified her life by choosing her wardrobe from just a couple of couturiers. She now has the confidence to stop experimenting with hairstyles and settle for what suits her face and her lifestyle best.

Of course, money does help, particularly in the initial process of experimentation. But in the end the Princess has settled for a handful of experts, all of whom are the best in their field.

Her clothes may be couture, but there are lessons to be learned from just how she wears them. She may have the best hairdressers in London, if not the world, but her daily hair care is easy to follow. Her beauty products are not by any means the most expensive. And, while it certainly helps to have the luxury of a personal trainer, finding a personal exercise routine and sticking to it is what counts in the long run.

The Princess of Wales has assembled a formidable team of experts on every aspect of beauty and fashion. Now you too can benefit from her discoveries. In this book you will find not only precise details of her metamorphosis, but also guidance from these royal advisers on how you can maximize your own potential in a similar way.

At the end of the day, there is no magical conclusion to this royal fairy tale. Princess Diana's transformation from plump teenager to the world's number-one cover girl and foremost ambassadress for British fashion was certainly no wand-waving exercise by a fairy godmother. Instead, it was all down to sheer hard work and will-power. Her determination to look as good as possible has helped her not only to achieve this metamorphosis but also to maintain it. Such energy and tenacity are qualities we can all emulate.

1
Closet
Secrets

*B*efore her marriage, Lady Diana Spencer, as she was then, was a working girl-about-town in London. She dressed informally, even for work, in comfortable separates. Dressing up meant something pretty for the occasional hunt ball or visit to Ascot. Suddenly, however, she was propelled into the heady but demanding world of the working royals, where looking good is a round-the-clock job – and where she has become the most photographed woman in the world.

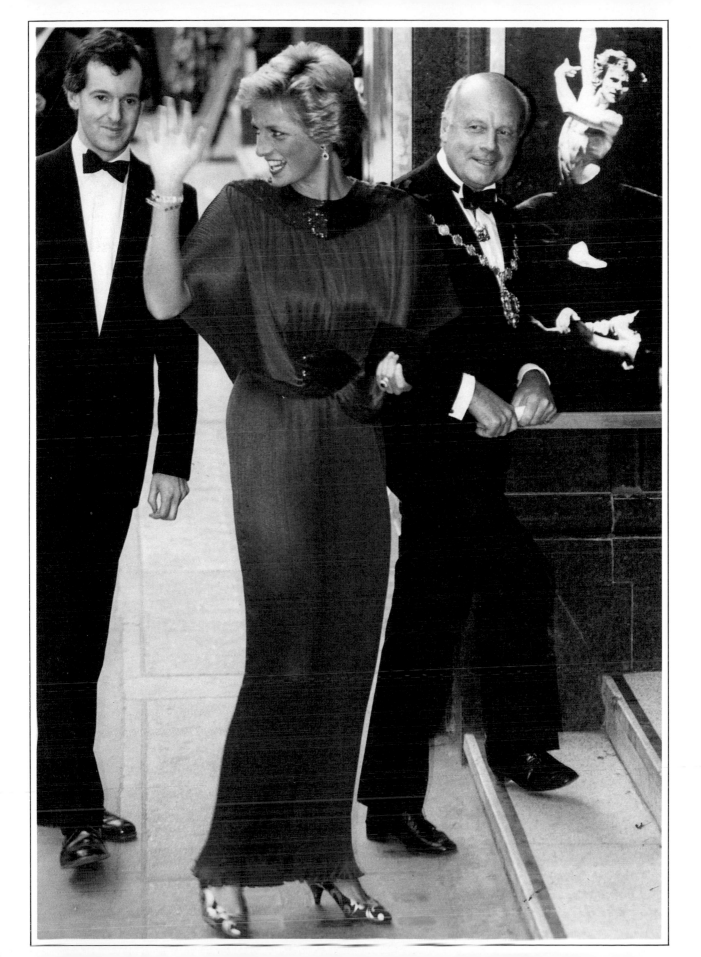

In the sort of circles that Lady Diana Spencer moved in before her marriage, clothes are not a priority. Among the English upper classes, there is a strong puritanical streak that baulks at spending money on clothes and certainly resists spending it on frivolous fashion.

This is a world in which clothes must not frighten the horses and must at all times be politely suitable for the occasion, be it the polo circuit or the hunt ball.

Fashion was not a priority for the country girl about town, moving in Sloane Ranger society. (Sloanes, or Sloane Rangers – the nickname for smart young people from the upper and upper-middle classes, for whom London's chic Sloane Square is the centre of the world – prefer clothes that are classic, conservative and practical.) Lady Diana's wardrobe consisted of simple, inexpensive separates, and when she became engaged, she was suddenly thrust into making major purchases which were quite outside her normal needs.

New fashion priorities

It might seem an enviable position to be in, but the clothes she had to buy were, in the main, clothes for functions rather than fun. Suddenly, she was in the public eye almost twenty-four hours a day and, worse still, every one of her first tentative experiments with fashion was made in public, photographed and minutely criticized by the world's press.

For example, when Lady Diana's engagement was announced and the engagement pictures organized, it was the first time she had needed a formal suit. On her mother's advice, she rushed into Harrods and settled for an unflattering, ill-fitting and ageing suit by Cojana. Its only saving grace was its bright cornflower-blue colour, which set off her huge blue eyes and sapphire engagement ring.

That engagement picture was to haunt the

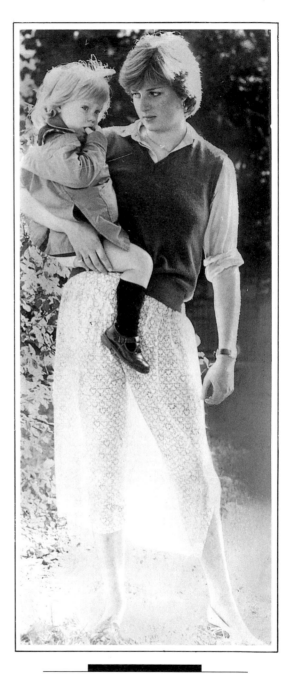

The world's first glimpse of Lady Di, the shy Kindergarten teacher who was soon to become the Princess of Wales. The photographers loved her bashful flirtation with the camera.

The fairytale princess on her wedding day in 1981 – barely twenty years old. Her romantic wedding dress of silk taffeta designed by Elizabeth and David Emanuel was criticized for its crushed skirt, which in fact added to her air of vulnerability.

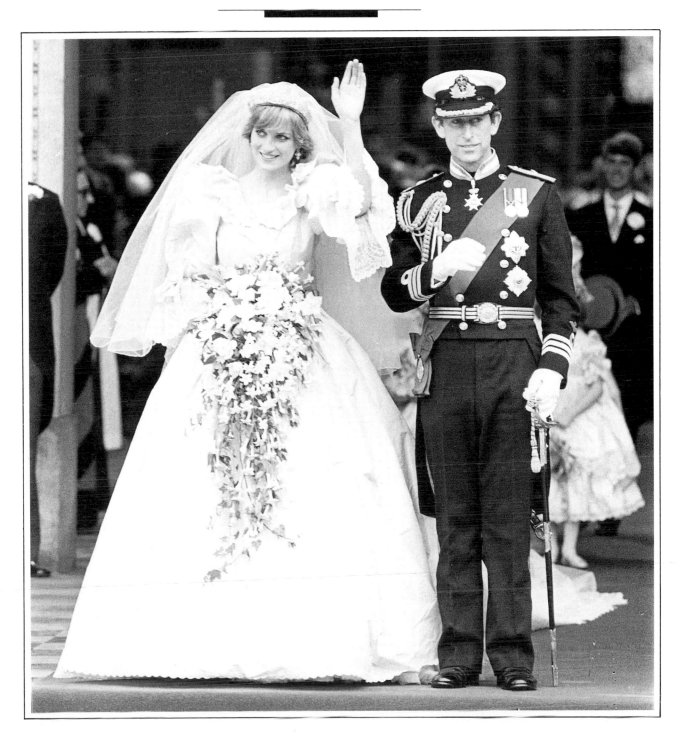

future princess from then on. It was one of the reasons for her determination to lose weight and generally improve her fashion image.

As a kindergarten teacher at the Young England School in London, Lady Diana had built up a simple, Sloaney wardrobe of frilly white shirts, corduroy knickerbockers and sheer, flowery voile skirts. These had enchanted her prince and her public but were deemed unsuitable for a future queen.

Diana's first Emanuel gown

Luckily, help was at hand. Diana's sister, Lady Jane Fellowes, had worked at British *Vogue,* and just before her engagement Diana had been photographed for the magazine wearing a blouse by David and Elizabeth Emanuel.

It was to the Emanuels that Lady Diana went soon afterwards for her first grown-up ballgown – the bravely bare, black, strapless style worn during her engagement for a visit to the Mansion House. The dress was sharply criticized by the press. Writing in *The Times,* fashion editor Prudence Glynn described its daring display of cleavage as "a frightful gaffe".

In fact, that sensational dress marked the moment that people realized there was a glamorous, sexy side to shy Di. Here was a newly engaged nineteen-year-old dressing for her husband-to-be, and it was the first sign that she was a fashion rebel who was going to make her own decisions. A typical girl of her age would probably have turned for advice to her mother, who most likely would have directed her into the safe hands of Bellville Sassoon, designers of dance dresses for decades of debutantes. Instead, Diana chose a dress with film-starrish glamour – daringly strapless and in black, a colour seldom worn by royalty.

Prince Charles reportedly loved the sexy black ballgown, so much so that it was to the then relatively unknown team who had designed it that Diana turned to create her fairytale wedding dress.

In the Emanuels, Diana had discovered a couple to whom she could relate. They were then in their twenties – not much older than she was – and Elizabeth Emanuel is, like Diana, passionately interested in dance.

The choice of the Emanuels seemed a good, if unexpected, one. This total break with tradition was what fashion pundits were coming to expect from the princess-to-be. Instead of trailing down the well-worn path to Hartnell or Hardy Amies, the Queen's dressmakers, or even to someone as fashionable as Zandra Rhodes, Diana was creating a style of her own. And David Emanuel's Welsh background made the choice a diplomatic move by the woman who was to become the next Princess of Wales.

The stuff of dreams

The dress itself established Diana as every inch the fairytale princess that her adoring public hoped she would be. No matter that the taffeta, spun and woven at England's only silk farm, Lullingstone, was a little creased, it only added to her vulnerability. The romantic bow-trimmed crinoline shape was the stuff of dreams and inspired a whole host of copycat versions within days. It was to dramatically change the way brides dressed for more than a decade.

But while brides all over the country were able to buy inexpensive versions of the new Princess's bridal vision, the exquisite detail of the original was impossible to copy. The ultra–heavyweight ivory taffeta was trimmed with Honiton lace and re-embroidered with thousands of tiny, mother-of-pearl sequins which Elizabeth Emanuel and her mother had sat up night after night sewing on, in order to preserve the utmost secrecy.

Soon after the wedding, the Emanuels

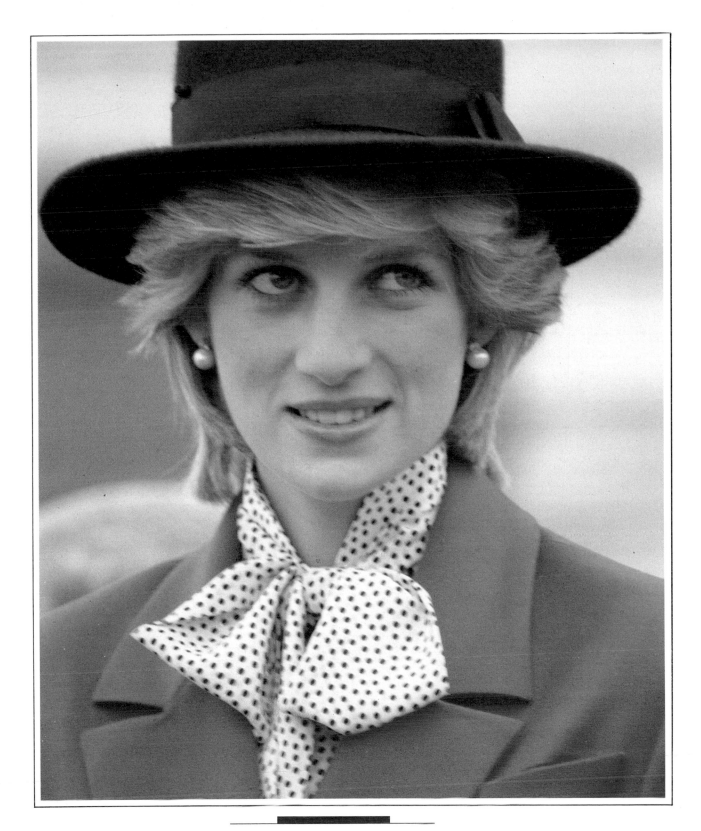

Early on, Diana made mistakes in dress: here, too much hair, too much hat, and a bow neckline
make her look older than her years. But she always looked endearingly sweet and pretty.

blotted their copybook by signing on with Mark McCormack, the super-agent who merchandises the stars. It was reported that he was getting them to charge vast sums for interviews and personal appearances. He was also arranging franchise agreements – soon after the appearance of the royal wedding dress came ranges of sunglasses, hosiery, perfume and bed linen.

The royal relationship cooled for a year or so, but Diana did eventually return to them, though the couple have now separated. While Elizabeth Emanuel has left couture to design for mail order and rock stars, David Emanuel is running a small couture business based in London's Regents Park and is again enjoying the patronage of the Princess.

The experimental years

After her wedding, Princess Diana continued to rely on *Vogue* for advice on building up the vast wardrobe that she was to need for her new life and its demanding regime of royal tours and public appearances.

Anna Harvey, then senior fashion editor at British *Vogue,* would call in clothes from a wide array of designers so that Diana could literally shop in private. At first, Diana was like a child in a sweet shop, wanting to taste something of everything. In the early years, it is almost easier to list the designers that she didn't patronize than to enumerate the names of those she did. Among her favourites were Bruce Oldfield, Jasper Conran, Arabella Pollen, Roland Klein, Jan Vanvelden and Benny Ong.

The British fashion industry loved it, of course. Suddenly here was a patron saint of British fashion – an ambassadress who could fly the flag all over the world. And every time she flaunted a new fashion, the cash registers started ringing.

First it was cossack-style hats and tiny feathered pillboxes, which went a long way towards reviving the flagging fortunes of the millinery industry. Then it was bow-embroidered tights, multi-stranded pearl chokers and flounced, lace-collared blouses.

For Diana, it was a learning process and one that she had to go through in order to develop her own style. But whereas other girls of her age could make their mistakes in private, the Princess of Wales's experiments had to be carried out in public.

Sometimes she looked ravishing, at times she looked old for her age, yet never once did she look bad. As one courtier close to her describes, "Right from the word go, she was confident of her taste. She has natural good taste in coordination, which is a real gift."

After the birth of Prince William, Diana bloomed with new self-assurance. Motherhood suited her and gave her new confidence. "Suddenly," says an insider, "she had blossomed into this fascinating woman."

Royal protocol

But while the public in general were beguiled by the Princess's glowing personality, radiant good looks, caring ways and dazzling smile, the fashion editors were less kind about her demure, spotted silk dresses and her fussy veiled and feathered hats.

It was difficult for the international press in particular to understand that, while most twenty-three-year-olds were free to dress in avant-garde, all-black, Japanese-style outfits or in baggy separates and casual styles, the young Princess was governed by royal protocol. She must always wear bright colours (except when in mourning) and a hat (even when it was not fashionable) and must never wear her skirts too short.

It was the hemline dilemma that was eventually to terminate Diana's long and successful

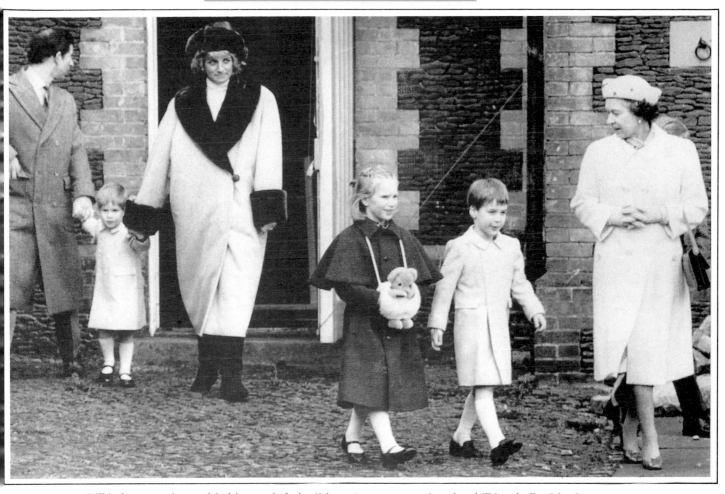

Still in her experimental fashion period, the Princess wraps up against the chill in a bulky fake-fur-trimmed overcoat. Nowadays she opts for sleek suits with thermal underwear beneath.

relationship with Bruce Oldfield, who had designed some of her most glamorous evening dresses. It was Bruce who put her into slinky, draped jersey gowns, many of which she still wears.

But as skirts became shorter, there was a continuing gentle battle between the Princess and Bruce over her hemlines. The Princess refused to wear very short skirts because she needed to be able to get in and out of cars with decorum. And Bruce, on the other hand, quite understandably didn't want his designs to look dowdy. Eventually, Diana, tired of haggling, simply stopped visiting his shop.

A sense of style

Today, the Princess of Wales has streamlined her look and her stable of designers. Like most fashion-confident women, she has developed a distinctive style which she sticks to. And while she loves to shop around when she has the time, she finds it simpler to rely principally on two British designers for her public wardrobe: Victor Edelstein and Catherine Walker.

It was fun when she was younger to buy off-the-peg clothes, like any other girl of her age; but as she has grown up, Diana has also come to appreciate the immaculate fit, perfect cut and quality of fabric she gets from buying couture clothes. Over the years she has learned only too well that, on the whole, the couture clothes she has had made look much better in photographs than off-the-peg clothes.

Couture clothes are made to the customer's exact measurements and cut first into a toile – a raw interpretation of the finished garment in canvas or muslin before the actual cloth has been cut. After this there will be at least two fittings to ensure a perfect fit.

Polished perfection

Of the tiny band of real London couturiers, Victor Edelstein is probably the one with the biggest international following both in Europe and in America, where he takes his collection twice a year. A perfectionist, with an elegant cut and sophisticated approach, Edelstein has a client list numbering not only several royals but an increasing number of powerful executive women working for huge corporations.

The Princess either pops down to Edelstein's small mews salon just off the Gloucester Road to view his new collection, or arranges to see the dress rehearsal of his twice-yearly show at the Hyde Park Hotel in Knightsbridge.

"We love it when the Princess does come to the dress rehearsal because it makes us get on with it," says the tall, intellectual-looking designer, who could more easily be taken for the conductor of a symphony orchestra. Designs from the collection are then adapted to the Princess's needs; for example, sleeves were added and hemlines lengthened for a trip to Saudi Arabia. Fittings take place at Kensington Palace.

"She's wonderful to design for," says Victor. "And I love the way she has now settled on this flattering 'Y' silhouette, with wide shoulders tapering to a narrow hemline, and finished off with a huge hat." The Princess knows that a widish shoulder line makes her waist look smaller, while the tapered skirt emphasizes her slim hips and stunning legs.

Slenderizing lines

A similar arrangement is made with the publicity-shy, French-born Catherine Walker, who works from a studio behind her shop in Sydney Street, Chelsea. It may be a coincidence that both these favourite designers are even taller than Diana, who is 1.79 m (5 foot 10½ inches) in height, and both understand how to accentuate her long slender figure and show it off to best advantage.

Catherine Walker's designs emphazise the torso with a flattering long line that seems to stretch the body and make it look even slimmer. And both Catherine's and Victor's ballgowns are beautifully fitted, with built–in boning that eliminates the need to wear a bra. In fact, the only underwear that the Princess needs under her evening dresses is a sheer pair of tights (pantyhose).

Young couture

More recently, Diana has also had clothes made by Tomasz Starzewski, a charming young Polish designer who has opened elegant premises in London's Pont Street, just off Sloane Street. The son of a Polish dressmaker, Starzewski specializes in young, fun couture clothes for the society set.

His brief curvy suits with jewelled buttons grace the best society weddings while his short, sassy ballgowns with their distinctive horizontal pleats dance the night away at all the glittering charity functions. (It was Starzewski who created the fur-trimmed, Russian-style wedding outfit worn by Victoria Lockwood when she married Viscount Althorp, now Earl Spencer, Diana's younger brother. This was how the Princess met him.)

By day, the Princess now dresses for

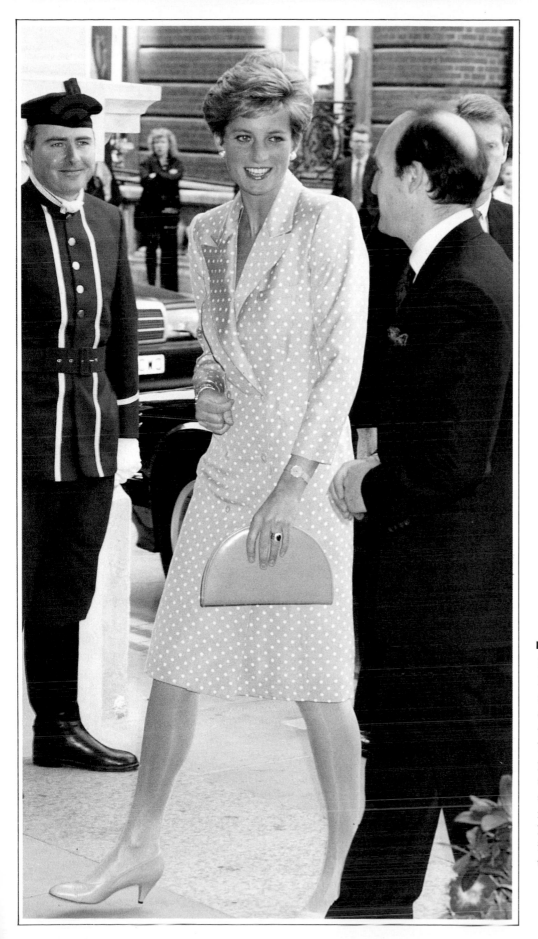

Pretty in pink. The Princess of Wales favours streamlined elegance for daytime wear. Here she teams a sleek double-breasted coatdress in pale peach and white spotted silk with a fan-shaped clutch bag and matching shoes in pink leather for a look that is coordinated from top to toe.

official functions in an almost uniform way. She wears tailored, streamlined suits in bright colours or two-tone combinations not so different from those worn by any high-powered executive woman – or, as has unkindly been suggested, by an air stewardess. The latter comparison has usually been when she has teamed these suits with pillbox hats.

Bold accessories

Diana wears fewer hats these days; they are now usually very large and without fussy trimmings. Many of her stunningly simple, large-brimmed shapes are designed for her by milliner Philip Somerville, who works from his

PLAY UP THE GOOD, AND PLAY DOWN THE BAD

- To minimize your height, Princess Diana's designer Victor Edelstein suggests choosing an outfit in two different colours that will visually break the vertical line, just as the Princess does these days. For example, she will wear a red jacket with a contrasting black skirt, or a sky-blue suit edged with emerald green.
- To emphasize your height, Victor advises using as few horizontal lines as possible, and avoiding belts or contrast colours so that the eye travels without interruption up and down the body. Now that she feels confident about her height, Princess Diana will often play it up in this way.
- Another tip from Victor is to always use a clever arrangement of mirrors to see yourself full-length from the back – a neglected and vulnerable area because there is so much of it on show with nothing to break it up visually.
- Diana's waist is relatively large but she makes it look smaller by wearing shoulder pads that are at least 2-3 cm (1 inch) wider than her natural shoulder line.

salon in London's Mayfair creating hats for most of the royal family and also for Margaret Thatcher when she was Prime Minister.

Milliner Graham Smith, who trained at the Royal College of Art and once worked for Lanvin in Paris, is another regular at Kensington Palace – so much so that his driver has become quite adjusted to waiting for Prince Charles's motorcade to pass by.

"What she buys has to do with a job," he says. "Like all the royals, she has a particular style of her own. She's certainly not in the business of buying a hat to say 'look at me'."

In the early days, Diana was self-conscious about her height and wore shoes with either flat or tiny heels, but she now loves the flattery of much higher heels.

The Princess also now has the self-confidence to do away with gloves (which she hates) for all but the most formal occasions, and even then she manages to give them a style of her own – like the time she teamed a long red glove with a black one to enhance her black-and-red Murray Arbeid evening gown.

She has also come to terms with the royal dress rules, learning that shoulder bags distort the silhoutte of her clothes, especially in photographs, and that it is better to settle instead for a tiny clutch style that can be tucked beneath one arm during all that countless hand-shaking.

Similarly, she has learned to avoid short, tight skirts that make it impossible for her to slide decorously out of the royal limousine, and she now has little weights sewn discreetly into the hemlines of full skirts so that they don't blow revealingly in the wind.

Personal preferences

Princess Diana has grown to love all those regally bright colours and uses them to her advantage, wearing sapphire blue, for instance,

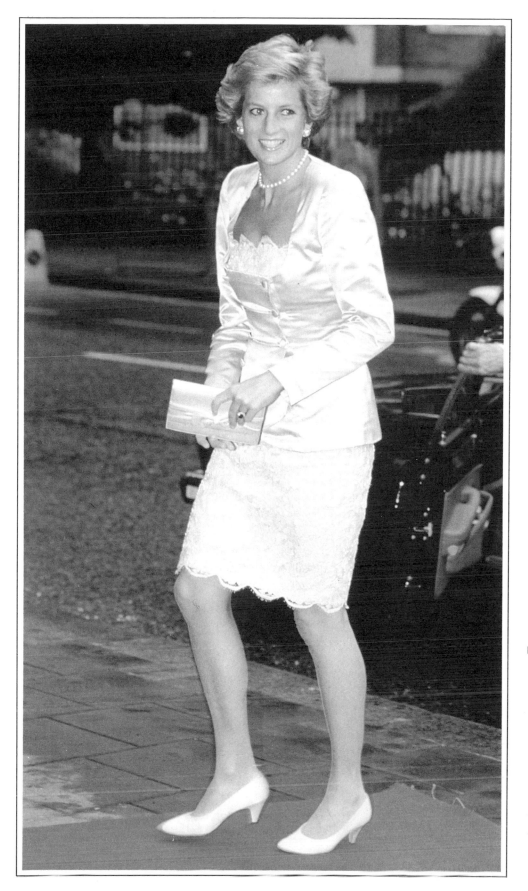

Princess Diana loves the pale and creamy shades that play up her golden hair and English rose complexion. Here, in a glamorous evening outfit that mixes different textures of flattering ivory, a satin jacket and lace dress are teamed with favourite pearls.

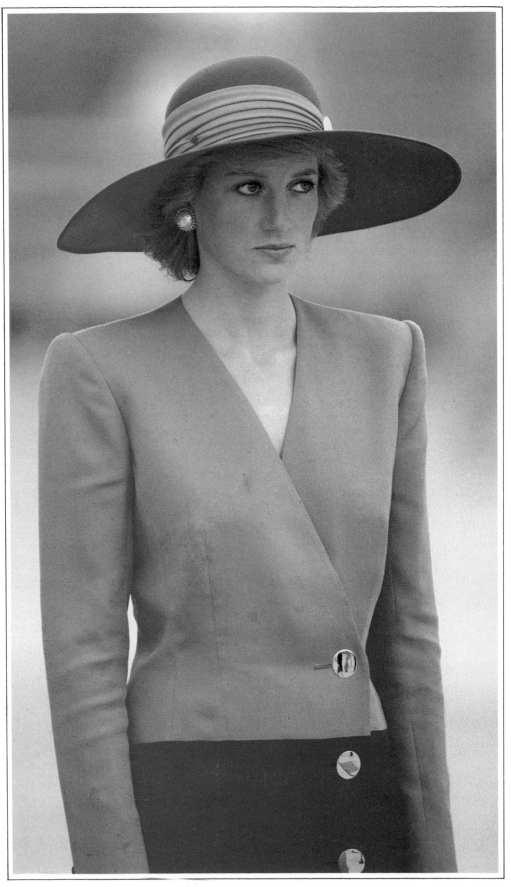

The princess has come to love those regally bright colours that help the royals stand out in a crowd. Here, shocking pink and lipstick red are mixed to stunning effect for an elegant coat-dress by Catherine Walker. The two-tone theme is echoed by a matching broad-brimmed hat.

to play up her eyes and her jewels. Bright scarlets and pinks are other favourite shades. Recently she has taken to wearing two-tone outfits, which help offset her height. She also loves creamy shades, which suit her English-rose complexion and golden hair. Black is reserved for serious State occasions or for night, when it enhances both her skin and her jewels.

After dark, the Princess prefers a long, slim, elegant silhouette, in strong colours, black or white but with very few embellishments of pattern or detail to detract from her glittering array of jewels. Many of her favourite evening dresses are dramatically one-shouldered – a line first designed for her by the London-based Japanese designer Haachi.

Privately, Princess Diana, like every other fashion-orientated woman with the money to spend on clothes, has a penchant for Chanel, Yves Saint Laurent, Kenzo and Valentino. But while she no longer actively promotes British fashion with an endless array of designer labels, she makes an effort to be seen to be wearing British publicly.

But there are exceptions. For instance, with her rebellious nature and sense of humour, she is drawn to the madcap Milanese designer Franco Moschino, who loves clothes with built-in jokes. He is not past decorating a dress around the waist with the logo "waist of money". This tongue-in-cheek approach definitely appeals to Diana, who buys his clothes off-the-peg from either Harvey Nichols or Browns in South Molton Street. However, it horrifies Moschino, who dotes on the royal family and feels that princesses should be dressing from couture all the time "rather than off-the-peg like an office girl".

The Princess wears her clothes by Valentino, Kenzo, Saint Laurent and Chanel only in private. But that original all-British

IN THE BAG

Princess Diana always takes one of her two faithful dressers with her on a royal tour. Her clothes are placed in hanging bags three at a time with their accessories and carefully labelled before being loaded onto the plane.
Lesser mortals, says royal fashion designer Victor Edelstein, would do well to bag their clothes three at a time into polythene bags and then fold them carefully into their suitcase, from which the garments should emerge creaseless. This is the way he takes his collection to New York twice a year, and he finds that, as long as the clothes are hung out overnight afterwards, they never need a press.

approach has now been played down by the Palace, who no longer issue details of the Princess's clothes because it was felt that avid interest in her fashions often diverted attention from the purpose of her visit. For the Nineties, caring is more important than clothes.

The Princess is also very loyal and supportive of those who serve her well. She sends Christmas cards to all her designers and has been known to ring through her good wishes personally to someone embarking on a new career.

The Princess of Wales feels the cold very badly and often asks for special linings to be sewn into outfits. Bruce Oldfield especially lined a cream suit destined for the chilly royal Christmas in Norfolk. And, from very early on, Diana discovered and extolled the virtues of Damart's thermal underwear, which enables her to wear svelte suits and silky dresses in all but the coldest weather.

Diana's leisurewear

The Princess loves swimming and has a vast collection of swimsuits. She chooses plain,

SUIT YOURSELF

Jantzen, the American sportswear giant, whose stunning, brightly printed bikini Diana wore for her Mediterranean cruise in the summer of 1991, have the following advice on choosing the right swimsuit for your figure.

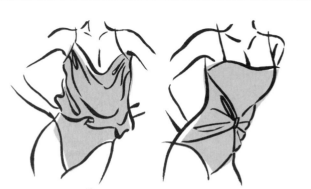

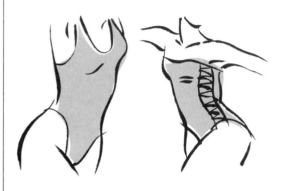

To disguise large hips, avoid tight belts and elastic that bind and create bulges. Seek coverage for the bottom and choose styles that pull the eye upwards, avoiding strong horizontals. Look for higher-cut sides, tied sides, skirted suits and side-shirring.

To flatter a full bust, pay special attention to comfort, support and coverage. Look for details that camouflage or pull the eye away from the bustline.

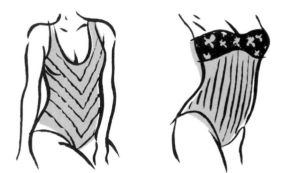

To flatter a smaller bosom, emphasize the contours of the bustline. Look for small ruffles, shirred or gathered effects, bright colours or dramatic textures, printed tops and mitred stripes.

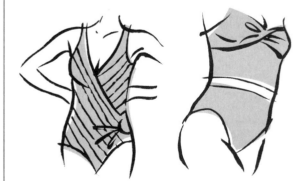

To minimize the midriff, fool the eye with fabric or styling that pulls the eye away from the tummy. Look for a suit with diagonal stripes, a high-waisted bikini, blouson lines, shirring on the sides or centre, mitred stripes, or styles with inner power-netting for tummy support.

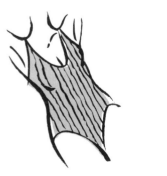

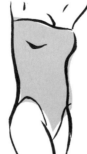

To make legs look longer, look for uninterrupted vertical stripes or prints, bare the midriff with a two-piece, or go for high-cut legs or side panels.

almost utilitarian styles for her early-morning swim, when she slips on a tracksuit over the swimsuit to drive to Buckingham Palace – but for holidays she likes fashionable prints for bikinis or one-pieces with matching sarongs.

The Israeli swimwear manufacturers Gottex have supplied much of Diana's most stunning beachwear, such as the ocelot suit with matching sarong which she was photographed wearing during one of her holidays on the Caribbean island of Necker. The brightly coloured bikini which she wore for her second-honeymoon cruise was ordered from the catalogue of the American manufacturer Jantzen.

The Princess has also sent sales of neoprene swimsuits soaring. This fabric – which is more often used by deep-sea divers and comes in fluorescent shades plus black – sustained a sharp rise in popularity after she was photographed in a stunning black and shocking-pink neoprene swimsuit.

Ironically, it is often when she is off-duty that Diana looks her best. It is, after all, a time when she can wear the sort of clothes that other women of her age-group wear most of the time. And after the formality, it's good to see her looking like ordinary young women in sloppy sweater and jeans tucked into boots to take the boys to school, in a Sloaney long skirt for the polo field or in a tuxedo for a pop concert.

The word "suitability" keeps cropping up time and time again. The secret of Diana's sartorial success is that she has learned to dress for the job – be it acting the glittering fairy-tale princess at a charity gala or popping into the supermarket like any other young mother.

The dressers

The wardrobe of clothes the Princess of Wales has accumulated, which was recently valued in excess of £833,750 ($1,500,750), takes a lot of looking after. Diana has two personal dressers, who look after her clothes and ensure they are all in pristine condition. Everything is carefully stored and card-indexed so that the Princess and her dressers know exactly when and where she last wore an outfit.

Often clothes are cleverly altered for a different look, not least because the Princess is always aware that she might be criticized for extravagance. On the other hand, when she arrived in Italy and wore a favourite old evening dress for La Scala, she was equally criticized. Consequently, her clothes are now very often carefully altered so that they look totally different. A pale-blue, long-sleeved, embroidered dress was altered to a sexy strapless number, for example. And often Diana will lend clothes to her sisters.

The royal evening dresses are dispatched to Tothills in south London for specialized cleaning and hand-pressing, at around £70 ($126) a time. Embroidered blouses and silk tops are washed by hand. Dresses are hung on padded hangers, and evening gowns have covers embossed with the Princess's cypher and made by royal warrant holders Eximious.

HOW TO STAND OUT IN A CROWD

- Wear vivid colours like scarlet, shocking pink or sky blue, as Princess Diana does.
- Add a stunning hat colour – which is coordinated to your outfit. Diana has discovered that large, simple shapes work best.
- Decide on the two colours that suit you best and then stick with them, advises Diana's designer Victor Edelstein.
- Never be dictated to by fashion – someone who has real elegance will take on board only what she likes and what suits her, as does the Princess of Wales.

2

Crowning Glory

A *hairstyle can make or break your looks. No one knows this better than Princess Diana. Ever since she brought the "Lady Di" haircut to the world, she has gone through periods of experimentation with her hair, switching hairdressers several times over the last few years. She has now settled for a style which suits both her formal and her off-duty lifestyles and which she can manage herself when necessary.*

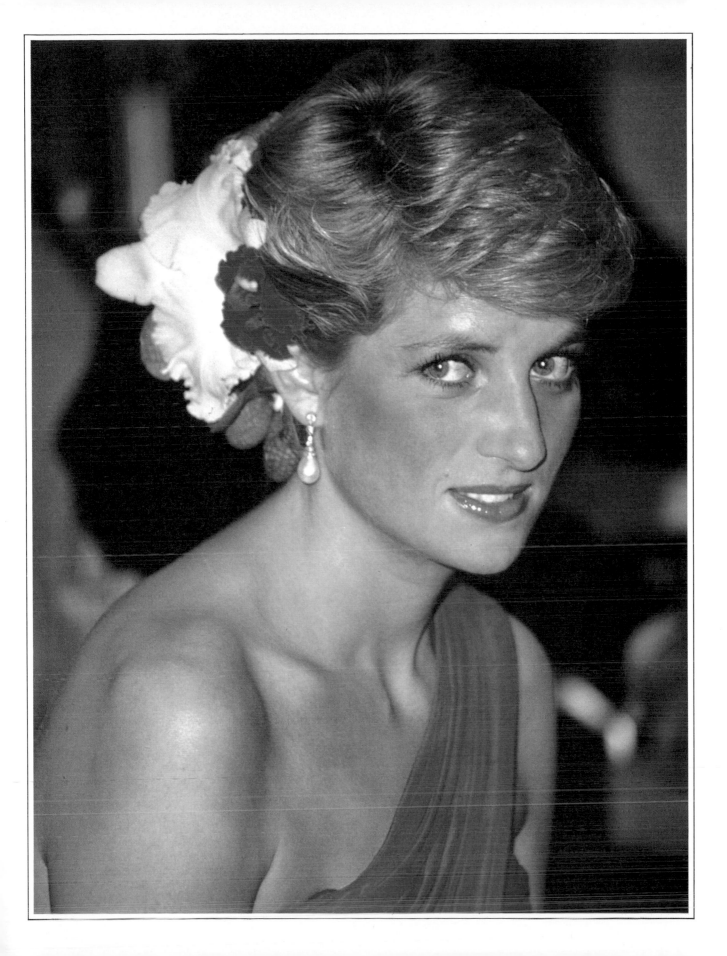

It was in late November of 1991 that fashion observers began to notice a growing likeness between the future Queen of England and the number-one super-model Linda Evangelista. The stunning British *Vogue* cover picture of the Princess in a simple black sweater by leading French fashion photographer Patrick Demarchelier provided the clue. Of course – they were now sharing the same hairdresser, international crimper Sam McKnight, who had given them both an almost identical gamine layered cut.

There were other coincidences too. It was discovered that both Diana and Linda use similar beauty products, even down to the very same rather offbeat brand of moisturizer from Boots the Chemist.

The only beauty secret that the Catwalk Queen and the future Queen of England definitely do not share is their hair colour. Evangelista is renowned for her ever-changing hair colour, which may go from brunette to platinum blonde to crimson and back again all in the space of a year, while Diana has stuck faithfully to her frosty blonde highlights for more than a decade.

Diana's muse

Most women with a strong sense of style have a role model on which to style themselves, according to the American fashion expert Eleanor Lambert, the guiding force behind the International Best-Dressed List. It is Linda who is currently Diana's muse. Through Sam Mc-Knight, a lunch was arranged by the then editor of British *Vogue,* Elizabeth Tilberis, so that Diana and Linda could meet and chat. It's no secret that the Princess would have loved to have modelled if life had turned out differently for her.

The Princess had briefly met Linda Evangelista and other super-models at the British Fashion Designer Awards about a year before this lunch. At that time, she had commented on their slim figures and guessed, more or less correctly, that they lived on nicotine. But she was longing for a real gossip. According to insiders they got on like a house on fire. Linda, like Diana, is a total professional who would be only too happy to fill her in on the tricks of the trade.

However, the *Vogue* cover with its Evangelista-style pose was in no way a deliberate attempt at modelling by Diana. The Princess had admired the work of Demarchelier, who specializes in photographing the world's most beautiful women and who had been commissioned by *Vogue* to do the earlier portraits of her wearing a satin sheet and a tiara and very little else. The Princess then commissioned him to do some pictures of herself "looking different" to give to close friends as Christmas presents.

Elizabeth Tilberis heard about the pictures and set about persuading Diana to let her use one of them as a British *Vogue* cover. It was not an easy task – the Princess feared that people would consider her vain – but she finally relented on the understanding that *Vogue* would publicize the Arts 2000 Year of Dance, the English National Ballet and London City Ballet, all of which Diana is patron of.

The super-models' crimper

The Princess may be a reluctant cover girl but she has plenty of knowledge of the glamorous international model set through the crimper she has had since July 1990, the Scots-born Sam McKnight, and his colleague, make-up artist Mary Greenwell. They travel the world with the top fashion photographers and their models, and as a result Diana now is party to all the fashion gossip, the hot beauty tips and the latest fitness fads. No one knows more beauty secrets than professionals like these, who

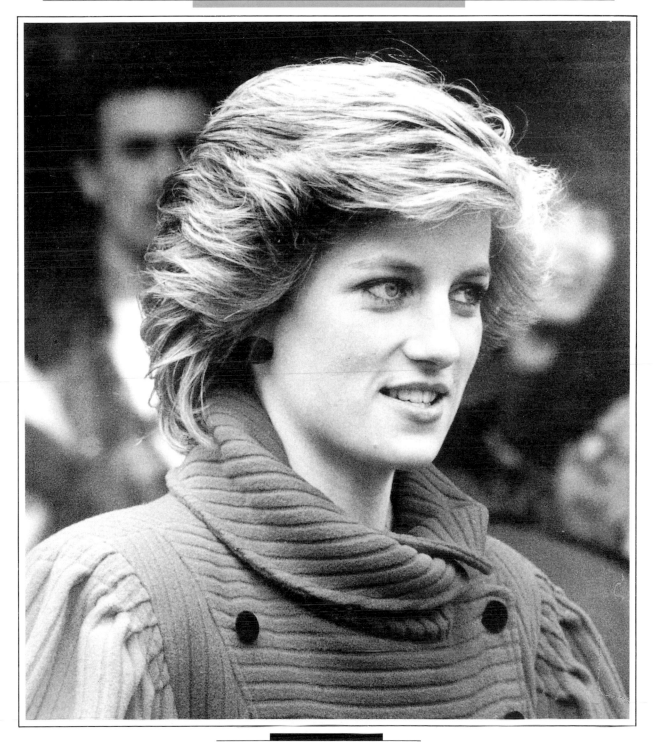

The original Lady Di hairstyle which was copied the world over. A soft fringe added volume and distracted from the Princess's rather large nose. When this picture was taken, Richard Dalton was still her personal hairdresser.

make their fortunes by helping models look better than they really are.

Sam McKnight is certainly no regular shampoo-and-set hairdresser. The son of a Scottish coalminer, he went to hairdressing college in Scotland and then joined London hairdressers Molton Brown before setting off to find fame and fortune in New York.

These days he commutes between New York and his flat in London's Docklands but always makes sure that he's free to fly into Lon-don once every six weeks to cut the Princess's hair. He will also accompany her on any major tours abroad.

Sam's philosophy is the total opposite of the Eighties wash-'n'-wear trend that took over the international hair salons. He believes that women's hair should look good twenty-four hours a day: healthy, glamorous and always well-groomed.

It is very possible that he may, in line with the other royal hairdressers, open his own salon. After ten or twelve years on the international circuit, a life of jetting off to another location almost every week and seldom having more than three weeks at home in a whole year rather loses its excitement. A London salon would certainly make him much more available to the Princess.

The relationship between any woman and her hairdresser is a close one. But the relationship between a royal hairdresser and his client is closer then most – if Sam is in town he will sometimes see the Princess of Wales twice a day, as well as accompanying her on royal tours.

The Princess is said to adore him. He has a relaxed and intimate way of gossiping and joking with each of his clients, which helps them unwind. Sam, however, will not be drawn on the subject of the Princess. He will gossip about anything else under the sun, but when it comes to his favourite customer, his lips are sealed. He, like the others that surround her, knows that just one indiscreet word could ruin this close relationship that he values so much.

In private, Diana will sometimes wear her hair greased back behind her ears for a very high-fashion look that she has picked up from Sam but which is decidedly un-Princess-like.

Frosty highlights

In between Sam's visits, the Princess either does her hair herself or has Karin Brown from

---

TOOLS OF THE TRADE

Sam McKnight spends his life travelling around the globe to do the hair of some of the world's great beauties, including the Princess of Wales. Here are the styling tools and products he regards as indispensable in his own suitcase.

- A selection of big round bristle brushes.
- Clairol covered hot rollers that do not damage the hair but give plenty of body and bounce. Sam was the hairdresser who pioneered the return of the roller.
- One of the new silicon serums like System Laminates Surface Polisher from Sebastian or John Frieda's Restructuring Serum. A few drops not only add shine but also help detangle and enhance texture by sealing the cuticle of the hair. "It makes the hair really shiny without being greasy," he says. "They're the best thing to happen to hairdressing since the invention of mousses."
- An old-fashioned hood hairdryer.
- Ultra-sharp steel scissors.
- Old-fashioned Elnette hairspray (or if he's at the ozone-friendly zone of Kensington Palace, Sebastian Laminates Spray, a quick-drying mist spray).
- BaByliss electric curling tongs.
- BaByliss electric flattening irons to flatten the wispy bits of fine hair around the face.

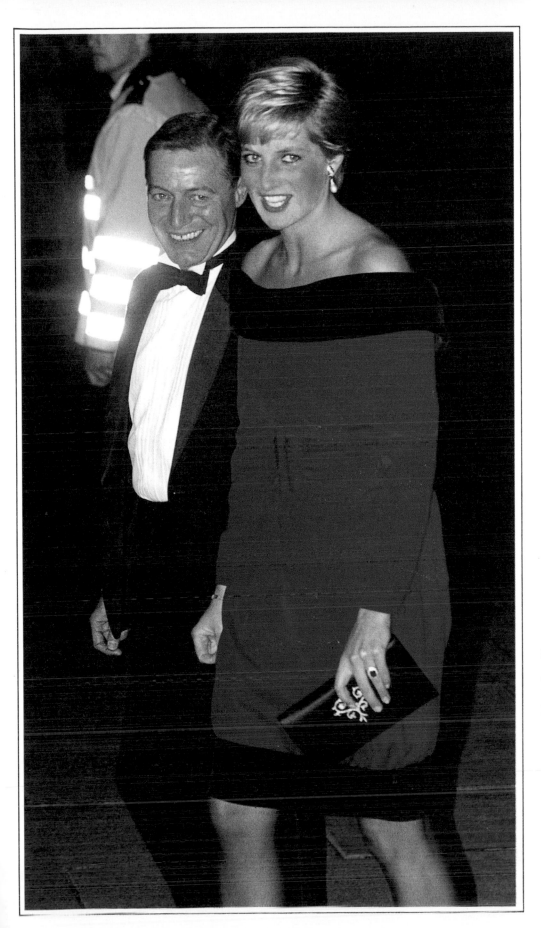

As the years have passed, the Princess's famous frosted highlights have become blonder and blonder. They certainly add glamour to the ultra-short style created for her by Sam McKnight, the international stylist who is now her regular hairdresser whenever he's in London.

Daniel Galvin style it. The frosty highlights are looked after by Nula, a freelance hairdresser who was trained by Daniel Galvin. Nula has been doing them for her since just before Diana's marriage.

Diana's natural hair colour is a mousy light brown. Then a few fine strands of blonde hair were introduced to give a subtly sun-kissed look. Over the years, more and more highlights have been added, using the traditional foil method, so that she is now almost totally blonde. She has her colour carefully maintained once a month. (Diana's highlights are too thick and stripey for Sam McKnight's taste, incidentally. He is hoping to persuade her to change to much finer streaks by adding lowlights.)

Daniel Galvin – whose salon in London's George Street is a haunt of all the best blondes, from Susan George to Pamela Stephenson – is the acknowledged world expert in colour. The stars think nothing of flying him across the Atlantic to do their colour *in situ*. It is Daniel's techniques – developed over the past three decades – that Nula uses on Diana's hair.

Natural movement

Currently, Daniel is advocating a "less is more" approach to hair colour, placing less importance on fashion colours, using less harsh chemicals and less solid permanent hair dyes, and requiring fewer trips to the salon thanks to a new programme of home maintenance. He uses a technique he calls "Natural Movement", which is a graduated use of colour combined with a shine-enhancing, semi-permanent vegetable finish.

The gentlest of permanent colours are selected two to five shades lighter than the natural hair shade and woven throughout the top layers. By using a minimum of two colours, hair appears thicker, more vibrant and full of light, with the true shade enhanced rather than

altered. A vegetable rinse is applied over the permanent colour adding additional shine and translucent colour.

Exposure to the elements, shampooing and styling products can dull colour, so Daniel has developed an at-home maintenance treatment. Something the Princess can use when she is away, it involves the simple and quick application of the prescribed vegetable rinse to brighten the colour.

Body and shine

Diana has also had root perms every two months to give her hair added body, making it easier to manage when she has to do it herself. The root perm gives soft fullness around the face that detracts in a flattering way from her relatively large and slightly crooked nose.

The shining condition of the Princess's hair is maintained by an intensive deep-conditioning treatment once a week after she has used her favourite Body Shop Camomile shampoo and Banana conditioner.

Sam McKnight has also introduced Diana to the Sebastian hair products from America which are used by the super-models like Linda Evangelista. A favourite of top session stylists is the Sebastian Molding Mud. This special combination of organic and synthetic resins alters the texture of the hair, making it softer and easier to style. It can be used on dry hair for instant styling or on wet or damp hair for a more sculptural effect which enhances the Princess's shorter cut.

The Lady Di hairstyle

All this is a far cry from the days when the then Lady Diana Spencer would pop into Head Lines salon close to South Kensington tube station for a quick shampoo-and-set by Kevin Shanley, her mother's hairdresser, who had been cutting her hair since she was sixteen.

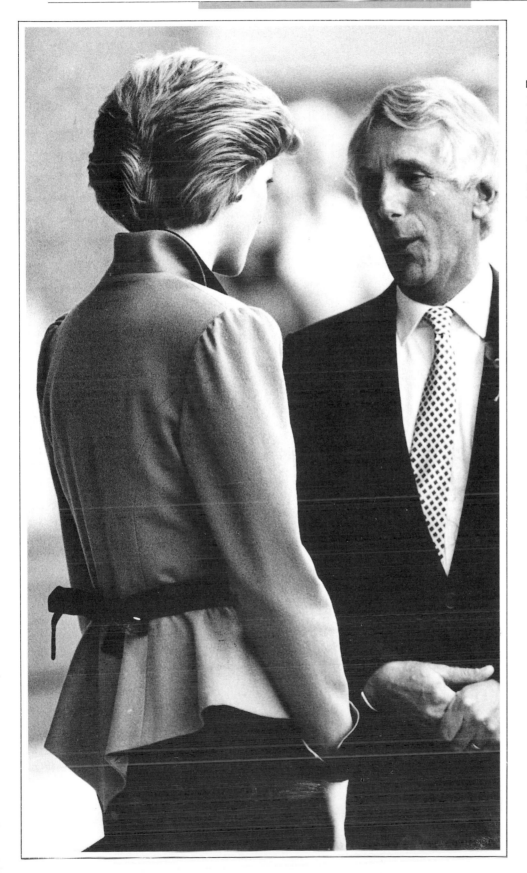

In 1986 the Princess's growing locks were being brushed back into a less successful "Teddy Girl" style, while root perms added volume and made her hair easier to manage on a daily basis.

ROYAL SOLUTIONS

Even Princess Diana has problems with her hair. Here is how she copes with some of the problems that beset so many women.

LACK OF BODY: Although Princess Diana has naturally thick, strong hair, she still likes to add more lift and volume to create height and fullness. While she sometimes has a root perm, she now tends to rely on a thickening spray applied at the roots and a BaByliss hot brush for styling.

MOUSY COLOUR: The Princess of Wales's hair colour is naturally mousy, a colour which can sometimes look dull, flat and nondescript. But, as Diana knows, mousy hair is also the perfect candidate for highlighting. A subtle use of fine lights can lighten and brighten the hair a little or a lot, adding texture and interest. Highlighted with hundreds of finely meshed streaks, especially around the hairline, mousy hair will look as though it's naturally very blonde. Highlighting is, however, a highly skilled technique, and kits designed for home use will not give such natural-looking results as salon highlights.

CHLORINE DAMAGE: As a regular swimmer, Diana needs to take particular care of her highlighted hair, which could easily develop a greenish tinge in a chlorinated pool (as can naturally blonde hair). She does so by applying a light coating of hair protector gel such as the one made by Daniel Galvin, at whose salon her freelance hair colourist was trained. This not only protects her hair but conditions it at the same time. Hair should always be shampooed after swimming to remove the chlorine; special anti-chlorine shampoos are available.

It was Kevin who had created the original and much copied Lady Di hairstyle of soft layers and casual face-framing fringe. And it was Kevin who did her hair for the royal wedding.

Kevin continued to care for the Princess's hair for years afterwards, sometimes sharing the job with his Scottish colleague Richard Dalton, who eventually became his successor in 1984.

Over the years, the Princess's changing hairstyles have been copied the world over. Ever since her engagement, hairdressers have been besieged with women bearing photographs ripped from glossy magazines with demands for the Lady Di look. In fact, in 1991 Diana was named as Head of the Decade by the National Hairdressers' Federation.

Federation spokesman Trevor Mitchell commented at the time, "The Princess is a hairdresser's dream and has been of amazing benefit to the industry – the best possible advertisement for the hairdresser's skills. And other royals could learn from Di. Most of them wear their hair too long for today's styles."

Initially, the Princess experimented with various styles with the help of Shanley, who would visit the Palace every morning to do Diana's hair after her early-morning swim.

Overtones of "Dynasty"

By the mid-Eighties, Diana's hair – by then much blonder – had grown considerably longer and was brushed back in a more glamorous bouffant style with overtones of the television series "Dynasty".

For the State Opening of Parliament in November 1984 she had grown it long enough for the much criticized chignon. Shanley had refused to do the chignon, believing that it would make Diana look too old for her age. He was right, of course. It was far too sophisticated for the then twenty-three-year-old, and the attendant publicity undiplomatically averted attention from the Queen in a way that it was not intended to do.

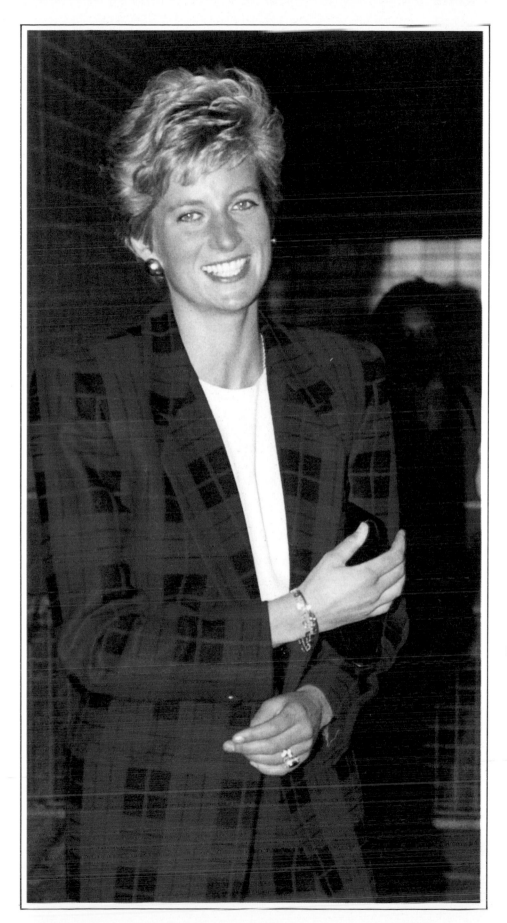

The Princess of Wales loves the short, urchin cut created for her by Sam McKnight in the hot summer of 1990. She finds it looks as good with tiaras and ballgowns as it does with her off-duty jeans and baseball caps. It certainly adds a contemporary informality to her workaday suits.

BRIDES' HAIRSTYLES

Denise McAdam, one of the royals' favourite hairdressers, is the acknowledged expert on hair for weddings, and has done the hair of some very famous brides. This is her advice on hairstyles for the big day.

- Don't dismiss short hair for weddings. The important thing is not to try to become someone different on your big day. The idea is that you should look like yourself but better.
- It is not necessary to put long hair up for a wedding. If it's beautiful long hair, let it show.
- If your hair needs perming, get it organized six weeks before the wedding. Colour should be done two weeks before the wedding.
- Always discuss your style in detail with your hairdresser well in advance, and arrange to have a half-practice. Ideally, show him or her a picture of your dress in advance and take the veil in for the practice session.
- Consider fresh flowers instead of a head-dress and have them wired up by your florist.
- If you are planning a country wedding without a hairdresser in attendance, enlist the help of your mother. No one knows your hair better. Just a simple braid or ponytail can look beautiful with the addition of fresh flowers.

It was at that point that Scots-born Richard Dalton, who had created the chignon, took over as Diana's regular hairdresser. Shanley incurred royal displeasure by selling the story of his days at the Palace to a Sunday newspaper, and Dalton left Head Lines soon after, setting up his own salon inside Claridges Hotel so that he could concentrate on looking after his royal client.

Dalton's mentor is the grand old man of French hairdressing, Alexandre, who looked after Princess Grace's hair. In his late seventies, Alexandre is still the most sought-after stylist at the Paris fashion collections, where Dalton is often to be found behind the scenes lending a hand. Always aware that she needed hair long enough for both tiaras and hats, Dalton would give Diana's hair a shorter effect she loved with the help of lots of hairspray.

As well as accompanying the Princess abroad on royal tours, Dalton became an almost daily visitor to Kensington Palace. He would set up his bag of tools in the royal bedroom soon after 7.30 am, when the Princess arrived back from Buckingham Palace after her early-morning swim.

Dalton became her friend and confidant as well as her hairdresser and was happy to indulge her constant demands for the changes which have saved her hairstyle from ever looking dated or boring. He even helped advise her on her clothes.

The Teddy Girl style

Not all his hairstyles were successful. That chignon, and also the "Teddy Girl" style adopted by Diana after her 1986 holiday, are examples of the less successful styles. In fact, Diana had taken the scissors herself to her overgrown locks and had rather overdone it. Dalton was simply called in to rectify the damage.

"I loved working for the Princess," he has been quoted as saying. "But it was twice a day, sometimes seven days a week. For eight years I never went away for a full weekend."

Going for the chop

The switch to Sam McKnight happened in July 1990 when he was called in to style the Princess's hair for a photographic session and ended up snipping off about 10 cm (several inches) during some of the hottest weather ever to hit London. Diana promptly announced, "I feel much cooler. My old hairstyle was a bit too hot for this weather."

At around the same time, Richard Dalton had hit the headlines with some unfortunate publicity about his sway at the Palace. It was reported that he had told the singer Dionne Warwick that he could enlist Diana's support for a concert that was raising money for Aids research.

Whether or not this was the reason for the Princess's switch of allegiance is not known, but shortly afterwards, it was announced that Richard Dalton was leaving his royal client to concentrate on his own salon. He has since closed the salon, however, and is based in New York, working for Clairol.

The job of hairdresser to Princess Diana is a demanding one. They are on call around the clock, usually beginning the day with a blow-dry at Kensington Palace at around 7.30 am. They are often needed at evenings and at week-ends prior to official engagements as well as for tours abroad.

Ringing the changes

The Princess of Wales does not feel duty-bound to remain faithful to just one stylist, possibly for security reasons. For example, Diana will sometimes enlist the help of Denise McAdam, who cuts Prince Charles's hair and is a regular visitor to Highgrove and Balmoral, where she snips the locks of most of the royal males. Diana will even pop into Denise's salon, Temple McAdam, for a quick shampoo and blow-dry with stylist Ivor.

The royal box

When Denise decided to open her own salon, together with Peter Carey, in Hay Hill just around the corner from Michaeljohn, she built a special enclosed cubicle for royalty. But when Denise realized she was expecting a baby, she felt she could no longer cope with the demand-ing royal schedules as well as a new baby while getting her own salon off the ground. She there-fore removed "the box", as she refers to the royal cubicle. She has a fear of the attendant security problems that are incurred with royals on the premises, and doesn't feel it is quite right for them to mingle with her customers. When Prince Charles suggests popping in to the salon for a quick trim, she raises her hands in horror and says "please don't". And she means it. She would much prefer to visit him at Highgrove (the Wales' country home in Gloucestershire), which she does at least once a month, although it is much more time-consuming.

HOW TO KEEP YOUR HAT ON AT ASCOT

The royal hairdressers are as adept at securing Ascot hats as they are at creating special hairstyles for their famous clients. Denise McAdam, who does the hair of practically all the royals, has the following suggestions about wearing hats.

- To make your hat secure, sew a ribbon or binding inside the crown along the edge. If it is a designer hat by someone like Freddie Fox or Philip Somerville, it will already have this.
- Hat pins are meant for decoration, not for holding hats on. Instead, pin your hat into your hair from around the crown using ordinary hair pins. "Four pins should do it," says Denise, "but I always add one for luck because I'm superstitious".
- It's not necessary to always put long hair up under hats – you can get away with different styles. The important thing is that the hat should go with the hair. The Princess of Wales has proved that short hair goes with virtually anything.
- Veils work best with a classic bob shape but pillbox hats can be very ageing and tend to look like part of a uniform.

3

Mirroring the Royal Look

*A*s far as Princess Diana is concerned, less is more
when it comes to make-up. She has now adopted the
fashionable natural-look face, which actually takes
considerable time and skill to achieve. She has also
rejected space-age technology in favour of a much simpler,
more natural approach to skin care.

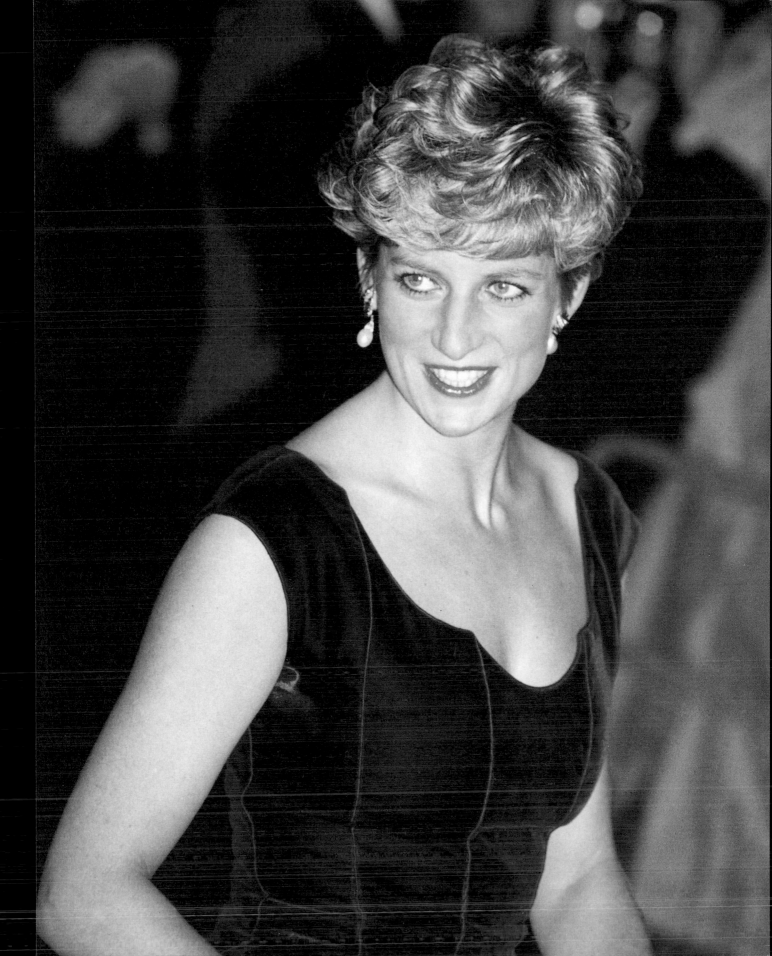

The Princess of Wales is surprisingly unpretentious when it comes to her beauty routines. Despite having the best of the new scientific skincare to choose from, she prefers simple moisturizers or French aromatherapy oils made from flower and plant extracts rather than products based on the new space-age technology.

And after several years of experimentation with make-up, she has adopted the fashionable less-is-more face. With the help of international make-up experts, she has learned to create the so-called "natural look", which is a great deal more complicated than it appears.

However, her real beauty comes from the inner glow of sheer good health that she has worked so hard to attain. Her healthy diet and stringent exercise regime do more for her complexion than the most scientific of high-technology skin creams or the cleverest make-up artist ever could.

Diana's non-made-up look

The picture of the Princess of Wales on the December 1991 cover of British *Vogue* magazine summed up her new look perfectly. To complement the gamine hairstyle by Sam Mc-Knight, his colleague, the make-up artist Mary Greenwell, carefully made up the Princess's face with the natural, non-made-up look.

Mary travels constantly, as she is much in demand with designers like Italy's Romeo Gigli and France's Helmut Lang, as well as Britain's Rifat Ozbek. She works continually with almost all the world's top fashion photographers, so no one could be more aware of the latest trends. She has even been hired by the Japanese cosmetics giant Shiseido to create a special line of make-up for them.

Mary first hit the fashion headlines with her innovative make-up looks for the Milanese designer Romeo Gigli and the Japanese

NATURAL-LOOK MAKE-UP

Most top make-up artists have a preferred way of doing basic make-up which will change very little from client to client. This is Mary Greenwell's favourite natural make-up routine, which is almost identical to how she makes up the Princess of Wales.

1 The base should be minimal for a natural look. Mary's favourite is Shiseido light Stick Cream base, which she also uses as a concealer, simply applying an extra layer under the eyes or wherever necessary.

2 Powder with translucent loose powder using a big brush fast and furiously all over the face. Using a puff makes the look altogether too powdery.

3 All you need for your eyes for the natural look, according to Mary, are two brown shadows. First, apply a soft taupe brown that is close to the skin colour on the eyelids themselves; a slightly pearlized colour makes the eyes look brighter and is easier to apply than matt shadow. Now add a deeper brown – five tones darker – to really bring out the eyes. Mary reckons that the Christian Dior shadows are the best in the world.

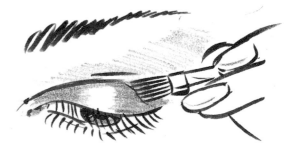

4 For the natural look, no liner is needed. "The fewer products you use, the better, and the more time you can spend blending them in subtly," she explains.

5 Use some of the dark-brown eyeshadow to make your eyebrows look thicker if you need it, but keep it natural and very soft.

6 Now apply mascara – dark brown for blondes or English Rose types, black for brunettes. Mascara on the bottom lashes is not really part of the natural make-up look, but it depends on your personal look.

8 Lips should be outlined first. Not only will it make lipstick last longer, but it also makes small mouths look fuller. The pencil should be a natural colour, slightly darker than your own lips. Fill in, using a lipbrush. Lipstick in a translucent grape colour will give the mouth fullness and sensuality.

7 Blusher is very important. Mary suggests that you look for one that is close to the colour your skin goes when it first catches the sun. She likes colours with a slight sparkle and recommends the Christian Dior or Bourjois ranges. The result should look like a natural healthy glow.

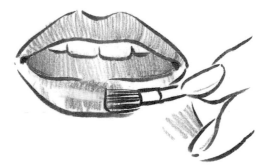

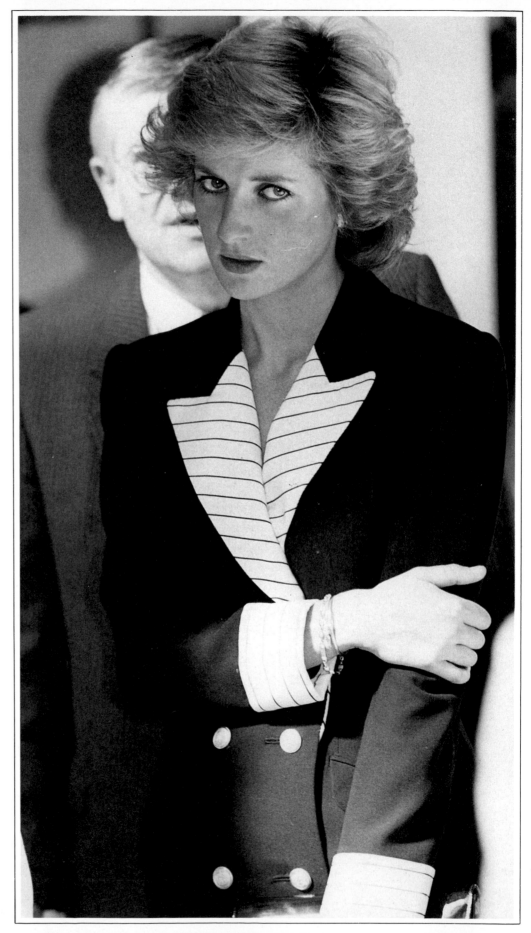

A time for transformation. As recently as June 1991 the Princess of Wales was still sporting her signature blue eyeliner, which she felt played up one of her best assets – her eyes – but her complexion is already touched by a much lighter hand. Her skin is paler and more natural-looking without the former blobs of bright-pink blusher.

designer Yohji Yamamoto. The new breed of fey, romantic models that both were using were ill-suited to the heavy-handed make-up of that moment. Mary's pale, ethereal faces hit the right key, and she has been hitting it ever since.

It is Mary who has finally managed to banish the dated blue eyeliner that Diana loved so much and which initially suited her so well. But nothing dates a woman as much as a ten-year-old make-up, and it is often too tempting to stick with the look one's husband fell in love with.

Now the Princess's eyes are subtly shaded with neutral tones of brown and taupe shadow, carefully blended using several different brushes, with the thinnest used instead of harsh pencils to delicately outline her eyes.

Her perfect peachy complexion is a work of art and far more subtle than her previous rather heavy foundation and over-use of blusher. She wears a light application of moisturizing foundation with built-in protective sunscreen, followed by loose powder.

A foundation just one tone lighter than her natural skin shade, carefully applied with a brush, conceals dark lines under the eyes and the redness to which Diana has become prone.

Instead of blusher Diana wears Esteé Lauder's golden bronzer both on the cheeks and around the edges of the face.

Diana's lips are fashionably paler and less glossy than of old. Outlined first with a natural coloured lip pencil, they are then painted with a peachy-pink lipstick applied with a brush.

The Princess's professionalism

The Princess is now most definitely locked into the international clique of fashion photographers, hairdressers, make-up artists and models that enable her to keep ahead of all the newest trends.

MAKING FACES FOR PHOTOGRAPHS

Making up for the camera requires special techniques. This is how Princess Diana's make-up artist, Mary Greenwell, suggests you do it.

1 Only use concealer for very tired-looking eyes or to disguise spots or red patches on problem skin. Using concealer under the eyes tends to accentuate crow's feet and make lines show up even more. Mary prefers to use a paler shade of foundation instead.

2 Vary the intensity of your make-up depending on whether it is for colour or black-and-white photography. Black-and-white photography demands a very even finish – perfectly flat with plenty of coverage – while colour photography, because it intensifies colour, calls for a minimal base.

3 Use a generous amount of powder for black-and-white photography, but for colour be very careful not to kill the natural skin tone – only use enough to get rid of the shine.

4 A natural make-up works well for both black-and-white and colour photography. Stick to browns, greys and blacks (the latter only for eyeliner and mascara) however much you like colour; these work best in pictures.

5 Concentrate on where you are putting your colours because a photograph will bring them out. Make the best of your features and go for a timeless look rather than a high fashion make-up. Blend your colours very well.

6 Don't forget mascara – it is important because it will "open up" your eyes.

7 Be very, very careful to keep blusher subtle. Don't use pink colours for colour photography because they will be accentuated. A healthy bronze blusher is better.

8 Don't use either very dark or very light lipstick. Instead, choose something a little bit darker than your natural lip colour, pencilling in your natural lipline first with a lip-toned pencil. Your lipstick should be slightly glossy to really enhance your lips and make them sensual.

Furthermore, she has mastered the art of applying make-up so perfectly that she does it herself for much of the time. Sam McKnight may be at the Palace every morning when he is in town, but Mary Greenwell certainly is not.

Many of the products the Princess now uses are identical to those of her muse, supermodel Linda Evangelista – who is such an expert with make-up that, unlike most of the top models, she prefers to do her own. Linda uses no "colours" at all – instead, everything in her brown-and-white striped make-up box from Henri Bendell in New York (all the top models have them) is confined to umpteen subtly different shades of neutral: black, brown, beige and white. And Linda never uses pencils, preferring to outline her eyes with a smoky ring of deep brown or black powder.

Natural-looking nails

For the *Vogue* cover, Diana's newly grown nails, which she is justly proud of and loves to show off, were carefully painted by Mary Greenwell with the natural-looking French manicure that the models love. Even this is much more complicated than Diana's usual bright-red nail polish.

It involves applying a protective base coat (the favourite base coat of leading manicurists and models is the American Develop 10 Program, which also acts as a nail strengthener). This is followed by a special opaque white polish applied carefully just to the tips of the nails. After that, a natural pinky-beige polish is applied and finally a transparent protective topcoat. (For full details of how to do a French manicure, see page 46.)

Once a nail biter of the worst degree, Diana has recently managed to grow her nails with the help of acupuncture and now proudly manages them herself most of the time.

Daly beauty

Originally, the Princess's make-up was created by Barbara Daly, the famous international make-up artist whom she met when, as Lady Diana Spencer, she was photographed wearing an Emanuel blouse for British *Vogue* magazine's feature on young aristocratic beauties.

The photographer was Lord Snowdon, who gathered around him his favourite team of hairdresser John Frieda and make-up artist Barbara Daly. On fashion sessions like this, assembling a team who get on well and know exactly what the photographer is aiming for is all-important. All three are quiet, unassuming types without airs and graces, and they did everything they could to make the shy nineteen-year-old feel comfortable and relaxed.

Diana was so impressed by Barbara's skilful but subtle make-up that she asked her to do her make-up for the royal wedding. Diana specifically asked Barbara for a natural make-up as close to her own complexion as possible.

Until then, Diana had worn very little make-up, and when she did she fell into the trap of using old-fashioned powder-blue eye shadow in the belief that it would accentuate her blue eyes, plus noticeable blobs of pink blusher on her cheeks.

Barbara showed her how a neutral-toned shadow in soft brown or grey would actually play up the blue of her eyes much more successfully. She also showed her how to shade her cheekbones with subtle rust and peach blusher to disguise their chubbiness. In addition, Barbara demonstrated how to apply concealer with a brush to subtly camouflage dark lines under the eyes and any blemishes.

Arriving at the crack of dawn at the Palace on the day of the wedding, Barbara waited for hours until the Princess was ready, rather than risk getting caught up in the crowds that were gathering in the London streets.

After the royal wedding Barbara continued to make up Diana for special occasions, but the Princess had learned so much from her advice that she was soon able to do her own make-up expertly in the space of about twenty minutes.

Barbara now has a very successful cosmetics brand of her own, called Colourings, which she runs with her husband Lawrence Tarlo, an American lawyer she met at a party following the royal wedding, held at the home of David and Elizabeth Emanuel, the designers of the royal wedding dress. The Colourings range is sold through branches of the Body Shop. Simply packaged and unpretentious, it contains many of the special products that are usually found in more expensive ranges. A number of the products are used by the Princess.

The secret of good skin

It was Barbara Daly who introduced the Princess to her special beautician, Janet Filderman. Despite the fact that Barbara is an experienced cosmetician herself, she had for years put her own skin into the gentle hands of this knowledgeable and experienced Yorkshire woman. Janet's unassuming salon in London's Wyndham Place, just north of Marble Arch, is a well-kept secret in fashion and beauty circles and has a steady stream of beauty editors, royalty and stars queuing for appointments.

Janet's philosophy is totally at odds with the approach of the cosmetics industry, which employs new technology to promote the sale of an ever-increasing range of complicated products. Instead, Janet believes very strongly in a less-is-best approach. She maintains that nearly all skin problems are caused by the over-use of beauty products.

Janet likes to develop a unique and special relationship with each client so that she understands the person's skin through their lifestyle, diet, stresses and strains.

NO-NONSENSE SKIN CARE

The Princess of Wales has discovered the benefits of Janet Filderman's skincare regime. These are the key elements of the programme.

- Invest in a good cleansing lotion or cream, but use a simple splash of lukewarm water instead of toner.
- Gently apply a good moisturizer in the morning only. You can also use it as an eye and neck cream, and a body lotion.
- If your skin is dry or mature, use a conditioning cream in the evening, but do not wear it to bed. Allow the cream to be absorbed by the skin for only ten minutes then blot off the excess.
- Never scrub the skin or squeeze spots. Most skin damage is caused by over-enthusiasm.
- Never venture out in the sun without some form of protection even if you are not actively sunbathing.

She is totally against the hype of the beauty industry and what she calls the "Dorian Gray principle" of the so-called miracle creams which are heavily promoted these days. She believes that skin-care companies should be encouraging the care of the skin rather than giving the impression that eternal youth can be obtained from a jar or a salon treatment.

Unlike most beauty practitioners, she maintains that the only products that are needed are a cleanser, one moisturizer and possibly a conditioning cream. Except in extreme cases, she is against the use of a night cream because she believes that the complexion benefits from allowing the skin to function without hindrance, renewing itself naturally during the hours of sleep.

She also knows that exposure to the sun is one of the most harmful things you can inflict on your skin, and begs her sensitive-skinned

HOME FACIAL

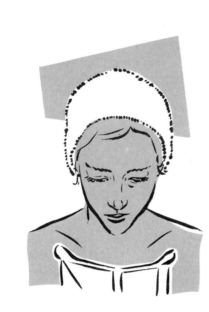

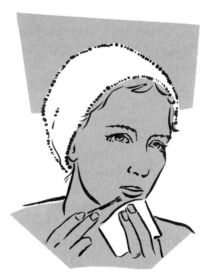

1 Once a month treat your skin to Janet Filderman's home facial. Cleanse, then hold your head, covered with a towel, over the steam from a facial sauna (or bowl of hot water) for a few seconds. (Do not steam face if skin is damaged.)

2 Use a blackhead extractor to gently remove any blackheads, placing the hole over the spot and pressing lightly. Work your way around your face and then dab each with a cotton bud soaked in surgical spirit (rubbing alcohol).

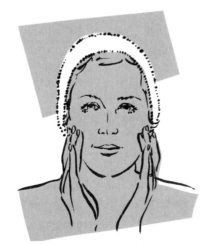

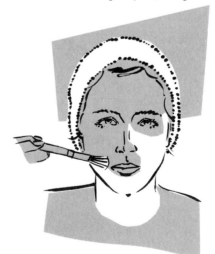

3 Massage in skin cream, beginning at the neck and working up. Around the eyes use circular movements. Finish off across forehead; repeat. Blot with a tissue, and remove surplus cream with cotton wool soaked in tepid water.

4 Mix 1 tsp Fuller's earth with distilled water to consistency of cream. Paint onto face and neck, avoiding eye area. Lie down with cotton-wool soaked in eye lotion on lids. After ten minutes, rinse off with warm water. Pat dry. Moisturize.

clients not to sunbathe and especially not to expose their faces, protecting them with a total sunblock. Perhaps that is why Princess Diana, though she still strips down to a bikini in the sun and loves to show off her bare brown legs, no longer has a deeply tanned face.

Contrary to the dictates of most cosmetic companies, Janet believes that special eye and neck creams and body lotions are totally unnecessary, as one good moisturizer can be used all over.

She also maintains that the fashionable trend for exfoliation (removing the dead surface cells of the skin with abrasive creams) is too harsh for the skin and exposes new cells prematurely. Skin, she stresses, must be treated with extreme gentleness.

Instead, she deep-cleanses the skin of the Princess and her other clients with a gentle method of vacuum suctioning to remove the impurities, afterwards applying a soothing and deep moisturizing mask.

Janet Filderman produces her own range of skin products which she sells to clients and by mail order. The Princess is particularly fond of the Milk of Roses cleanser.

The well-conditioned face

Another of the Princess's sources of expert advice on skin care is Mary Greenwell, her make-up artist, who has very definite ideas on the subject and is well-informed through her contacts with leading cosmetics houses.

Mary stresses the importance of a healthy diet and plenty of sleep, and she believes that the most important starting point for any make-up is a well-conditioned face. She recommends using an eye cream from a young age, and a rich neck cream from the mid-thirties – in other words, before the damage is done. She also advises that a repair lotion be worn under daytime moisturizer from the mid-thirties. Her favourite products are from Shiseido, Estée Lauder, Clarins and La Prairie.

Although much of Mary Greenwell's advice is contrary to Janet Filderman's counsel, in the end the Princess will no doubt follow whichever recommendations she finds are best for her own skin.

Seeing red

While the Princess is generally credited with a flawless skin, close observers have noticed a recent tendency to the redness and breakouts normally associated with rosacea.

Rosacea is a common problem with the sort of delicate English rose complexion that the Princess has. The condition is characterized by acute flushing accompanied by broken capillaries, swelling and sometimes a rash of tiny bumps and pustules. These are quite easily camouflaged with concealing creams and good make-up, but are nonetheless annoying for a young woman who takes such meticulous care of her skin. Rapid temperature changes, sunlight, spicy food, very hot drinks and alcohol can all aggravate the problem, but a major factor is usually emotional stress.

Holistic skin care

Holistic beauty practitioner Bharti Vyas is one of the few experts who can help rosacea sufferers. It is quite likely that the Princess will visit her tiny Chiltern Street salon, where customers include a steady stream of beauty writers, fashion designers and the Princess's own hairdresser Sam McKnight.

It is said that Diana is already using some of Bharti's products, like the Skin Softener, an all-purpose petroleum-based cream that can be used as eye-make-up remover, face make-up remover, skin softener for both face and body, cleanser and bath oil.

Bharti believes that stress-related rosacea is

caused by the blockage of lymph glands, and she cures this slowly but effectively in several ways. First, she puts the sufferer on a gluten-free diet which excludes dairy or wheat products that clog up the system, and reduces intake of red meat. Then she does a form of zone therapy, applying magnetic electrodes to the ear. She completes her treatment with a gentle but thorough facial, which again focuses on the lymph glands to leave the skin remarkably unflushed.

Patients usually start with an intensive course of weekly treatments for the first three months, after which monthly visits are generally sufficient.

As this is a stress-related skin problem, Bharti would also recommend that the Princess relax at bedtime by soaking in a deep, hot bath in which have been dissolved several handfuls of Dead Sea Salts – mineral-rich crystals from

the Dead Sea. They not only have an immensely soothing effect but are said to improve the circulation and stimulate the lymph system.

Aromatic oils

Another holistic beauty treatment the Princess has tried is aromatherapy, based on the use of essential oils extracted from certain plants.

She is a particular fan of the aromatherapy oils produced by leading aromatherapist Danièle Ryman, who massages the rich and famous at her salon in Mayfair's Park Lane Hotel. Diana uses the oils at home to help her relax, not only dropping them into her bath water and using them for soothing body lotions but also diffusing them onto her table lamps so that they fill her rooms with a calming ambience. When she is suffering from jetlag, she uses, like many other celebrities, Danièle Ryman's Anti-Jetlag kit. It contains a tingling gel to clear the sinuses, and orange oil to promote sleep.

Prince Charles too is knowledgeable about aromatherapy and adds extracts of nerve-calming rosemary and relaxing lavender to his bath water. He hopes to produce both scent and aromatherapy oils from flowers grown at Highgrove, to give as gifts to friends and family.

There are between 200 and 300 different aromatherapy oils in use. Those said to be relaxing include camomile, orange blossom, lavender, rose and sandalwood, while oils regarded as stimulating include peppermint, rosemary and basil.

Favourite beauty products

Another product on the Princess's dressing table is Lilyroot and Marshmallow moisturizing lotion from Boots; this is also super-model Linda Evangelista's favourite. It is only sold in their stores as part of a gift pack, but Boots continue to make special supplies for the Princess.

FRENCH MANICURE

The Princess of Wales enjoys playing up her newly grown-out nails with a French manicure. Here is how to do it yourself.

1 Remove old varnish with remover on cotton wool. Soak hands in a small bowl of warm water mixed with a little facial wash for three minutes, then brush the nails with a bristle brush. Dry with a soft towel.
2 Apply cuticle cream to the base of each nail and massage it in. Gently push back the cuticles with a cotton bud. Shape the nails with an emery board then wipe to remove excess cream.
3 Apply a protective nail base.
4 Apply a narrow line of opaque white nail polish to the tips of the nails, tidying mistakes with remover on a cotton bud.
5 Apply two coats of pale pinky-beige polish.
6 Apply a clear protective top coat and allow to dry for at least twenty minutes.

Diana developed a liking for the Clarins skin-care products, which she was introduced to on a visit to Champneys health farm. She uses their day and night creams, Alpine herb cleanser and yellow toner, all from the Sensitive Skin range.

And she is a great fan of the inexpensive Body Shop ranges. She uses their Milk Bath, Strawberry Body Shampoo, Elderflower Water Skin Tonic and Elderflower Eye Gel for soothing tired eyes and reducing puffiness. In addition she buys their Rich Night Cream with Vitamin E, and she soothes her feet with their Peppermint Foot Lotion.

It has also been reported that the Princess has experimented with the Erno Laszlo skin products. Erno Laszlo was a famous American beautician who based his skin-care range on very thorough cleansing of the skin using a special black mud soap and splashing the face with cold water several times twice a day. The ritual becomes something of a religion with its disciples, who include any number of celebrities. The regime is available as part of a club membership through stores such as Harrods.

Passion for perfume

The Princess's long-time favourite scent is Diorissimo, a fresh, flowery lily-of-the-valley perfume. She has also recently discovered Annick Goutal's Passion, a haunting blend of tuberose and jasmine from Grasse mixed with vanilla.

This little-known and rather elitest French perfume range is something of a cult among stars like Madonna and perfume connoisseurs. It was at one time only available in Annick Goutal's Paris boutiques, but now the Princess can buy it in London from Harrods, Selfridges and Fortnum & Mason. Its creator, Annick Goutal, was originally a gifted musician and fashion model who started her own perfume house in 1980; she was one of the few women

to succeed in the heady and competitive world of Paris perfume.

As well as Passion perfume in its beautiful round, translucent glass bottle topped with its signature golden butterfly stopper, there are matching Passion perfumed pebbles to heat on a lamp and scent a room.

ROYAL BEAUTY SECRETS

- Royal beauties cannot be forever reapplying lipstick – they put it on in such a way that it will last. Here's how it's done. First, when you are putting on your foundation and powder, apply them to your lips too, to provide a good base for the lipstick. Next, outline lips with a lip pencil that is as close to your natural lip colour as possible, no matter what colour lipstick you are using. Blend softly with a brush. Fill in lip colour with a lip brush, then simply hold a tissue on them for a second without properly blotting. Alternatively, blot (and, if desired, powder) lips then apply a second coat and blot it very lightly.
- Diana is now wearing the pale pink and nude-toned lipsticks fashionable among models. She likes Clinique's Roseberry Stain, a soft but bright pink which flatters her English rose complexion.
- Don't succumb to the vogue for corrective colour creams and powders. Mary Greenwell advises Princess Diana against the conventional wisdom that suggests using a green base to offset her tendency to high colour. Nor is Mary in favour of concealer creams, despite Diana's tendency to blotchiness. Instead, she prefers to use a paler shade of a good foundation.
- Blusher must look natural. It was Barbara Daly who steered Diana away from harsh blobs of pink and showed her how to use soft peach and rust instead. Today Diana favours golden bronzing powder for a really subtle effect.

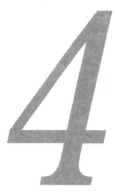

Inside the Royal Jewel Box

*W*ith *a bounty of real jewels to choose from, the Princess of Wales might seem to be spoiled for choice. In fact, she often prefers to shop for fashionable faux pearls and diamonds instead of raiding the royal vaults. And when she does delve into the vast and dazzling collection of royal jewels, she has fun wearing them in different ways.*

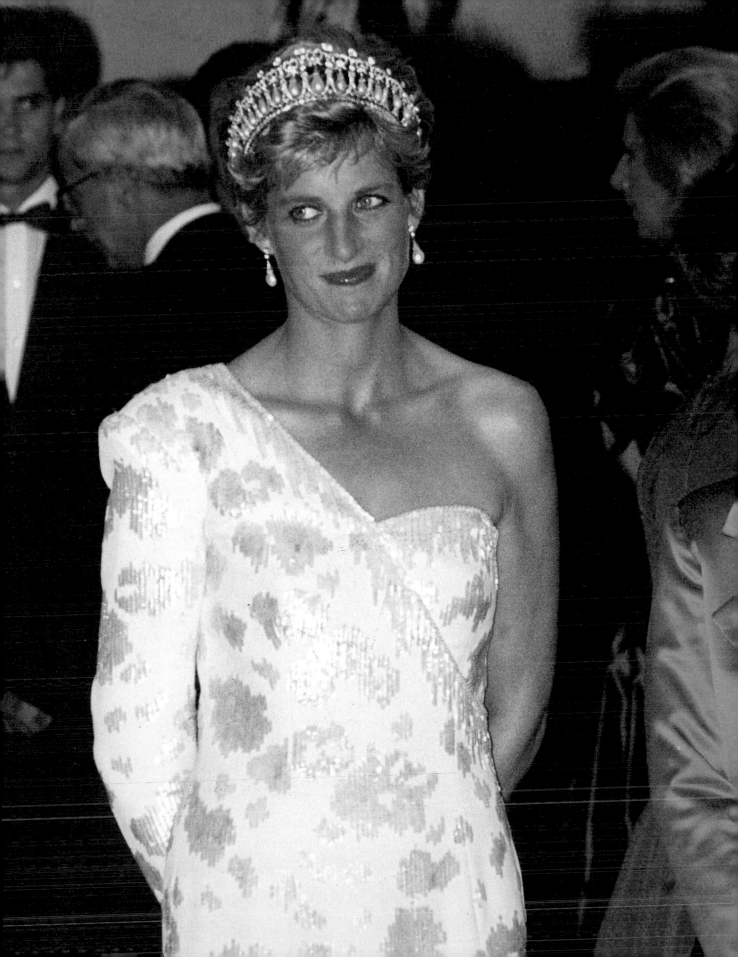

Although the future Queen Diana of England stands to inherit the most shining collection of jewellery in the world, the jewels she most enjoys wearing come not from the royal vaults, but from a very different treasure trove that anyone can wander into, in London's Fulham Road. It's a fashionable costume jewellery shop called Butler & Wilson, which is a favourite haunt not only of Diana but of all the young royals.

This is where the Princess will stop off unannounced to buy, for example, Chanel-style pearl earrings with twisted gilt edging for herself or glittery spider brooches for her friends.

Jewellery hi-jinks

She also enjoys passing off some of their jewellery as the real thing. For example, on one occasion she wore some spectacular star-and-moon earrings from Butler & Wilson on a royal tour to Saudi Arabia, and the entire press corps were fooled into assuming that they were a lavish present from her host. Instead of the small fortune that these crescent moons (Saudi Arabia's national symbol) would have cost in diamonds, the Princess bought them herself from Butler & Wilson for just £46 ($83) the day before she left for the Gulf.

Another time, for a State visit to Italy she wore diamanté bow-and-heart earrings that the Italians thought came straight out of the vaults at Buckingham Palace.

Young and fun

She has also sported a Butler & Wilson diamanté snake pin on the lapel of her dinner jacket and pinned one of their huge glittery star brooches onto the hip of her evening dress.

Young and fashionable, this is the sort of jewellery she can have real fun wearing, and, at the end of the day, it doesn't need to be put back in the safe.

The Princess of Paste

Nicky Butler and Simon Wilson, known in the fashion business as the Princes of Paste or the Kings of Diamanté, first set up shop with a stall in west London's Portobello Road antique market twenty-one years ago, later moving to the Antiquarius market in the Kings Road at the height of the Swinging Sixties.

Instead of the dayglo plastic jewellery that was currently fashionable, they offered their own unique selection of old, but inexpensive, pieces picked up in antique markets. Carefully restored and polished and laid out to look like fashion jewellery, these pieces soon became the height of fashion.

They stocked Art Deco brooches in Bakelite, bronze hand pins, butterfly wing pendants and ivory necklaces, all of which became so fashionable that they resorted to making copies of things they could no longer find.

High fashion

Today, Butler & Wilson have several shops of their own, in London, Glasgow and Los Angeles, plus others within stores. They produce twice-yearly collections of their own high-fashion designs, such as the jewel-coloured Venetian glass necklaces.

As well as royalty, their starry clientele includes Faye Dunaway, Lauren Hutton and Catherine Deneuve, to name just a few. Elton John is particularly partial to their diamanté teddy-bear cufflinks with fake ruby bow-ties, which he likes to give as presents. With prices starting at under £20 ($36), it's the place where practically anybody can afford some royal jewels.

Before her marriage, Princess Diana's jewel box was practically empty. There was the gold chain with the initial "D" hanging from it, which was a leaving present from her friends at West Heath School. There was the twisted

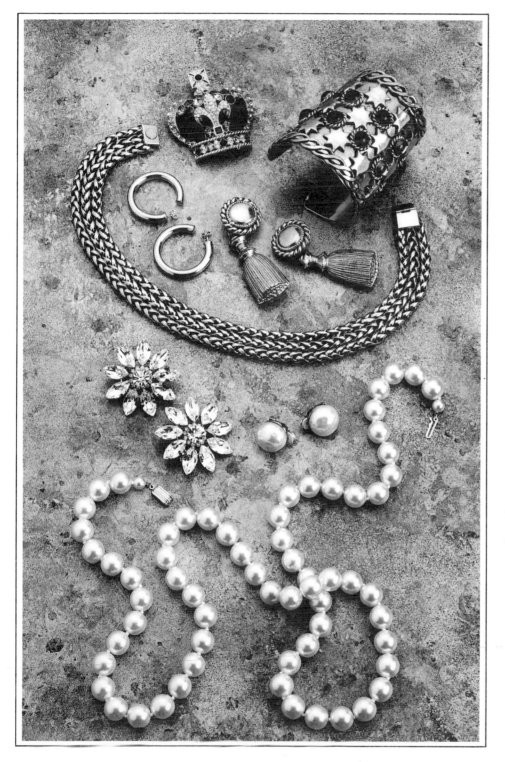

AFFORDABLE JEWELLERY

Butler & Wilson, the costume-jewellery shop patronized by the Princess of Wales and other young royals, sells jewellery well within the financial reach of ordinary mortals They suggest that the following pieces will be both affordable and versatile.

- A pair of pearl stud earrings, with matching rope long enough to twist into a double necklace. Pearls flatter the skin, can be worn formally or informally and look good with almost everything.

- A talking-point brooch like Diana's glittery spiders and lizards. "A brooch like this goes on for ever and adds interest to the plainest clothes," says Simon Butler.

- A nice chunky chain bracelet or a big silver or gilt cuff to wear with sweaters.

- A pair of plain silver hoop earrings to go with everything.

- An essential pair of important-looking gold drop earrings, perhaps with tassels.

- An inexpensive antique-look three-strand gilt necklace.

- A wonderful pair of diamanté earrings for evening.

- A long pearl rope to wear with pearl earrings or alone.

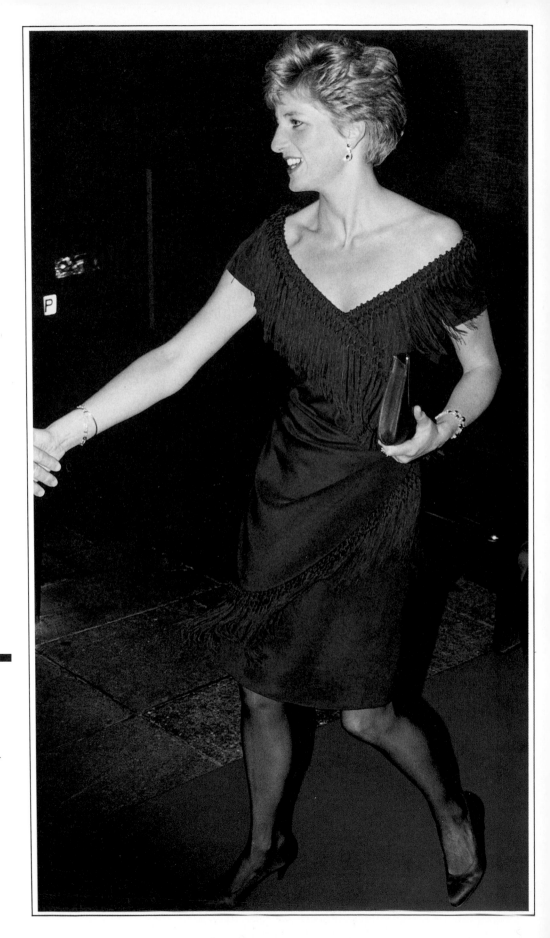

Princess Diana loves
sapphires, which echo
the colour of her eyes.
Her engagement ring,
consisting of a huge
sapphire surrounded by
diamonds, set a trend
among brides-to-be.
Here she develops the
theme with a sapphire-
and-diamond bracelet
and earrings.

Russian wedding ring that she wore on a little finger, and a silver bracelet with hearts on it, but that was about all.

The family tiara

Of course, there was the Spencer family jewel-pool which she shared with her sisters, her mother Mrs Shand Kydd and her grandmother Lady Fermoy. And it was from this shared jewel-pool that she borrowed the dainty tiara of diamond fleurettes that she wore on her wedding day, just as her sister Jane had before her. With it she wore diamond earrings borrowed from her mother.

Later in the day, when she went off on her honeymoon dressed from head to toe in sunny apricot, she wore the Spencer family pearl choker that had been clasped around her sister's neck at the service itself.

The choice of the pretty but modest Spencer family tiara, instead of the lavish diamond-and-pearl tiara that the Queen had just given her, surprised insiders. But for a twenty-year-old with a short, shaggy hairstyle complete with fringe, it was a more suitable and comfortable choice. For the most important day of her life, Diana, quite rightly, didn't want to change the sweet young look that had captured her prince.

Later on, when she became more accustomed to her tiara lifestyle, she was to grow her hair longer and also, on more than one occasion, have it put up into a chignon. (But, ironically, neither style was as successful as her gamine short cut, which works as well with grand jewels on State occasions as it does with baseball cap and jeans.)

Tiaras must be fixed by a skilful and experienced hairdresser. It is for this reason that on grand-occasion days, the royal ladies can be found at teatime in Kensington Palace wearing casual clothes but with newly placed tiaras on

COPING WITH A TIARA

Tiaras can be both uncomfortable and heavy, depending on the style and the number of jewels. "To wear a tiara well it has to be very well attached – tiaras definitely shouldn't be worn to fool around in," says hairdresser Denise McAdam, who is well used to royal tiaras. "It's just like walking round with three books on top of your head."

- "The secret of wearing a tiara successfully lies in the pins," adds Denise, who learned the technique from Princess Grace when she did her hair as a junior in Edinburgh. "I always believe you should use as few as possible. The first one should 'catch' and hold the tiara in place with the hair very slightly twisted onto it. If they feel a bit of pain, it's working."
- Always backcomb hair before attaching a tiara. You will need a bit of padding to hold it in place.
- Don't, whatever you do, ever get hairspray on the jewels.

their heads. Tiaras are deceptively heavy, and many is the royal lady who ends the night with a blinding headache.

Showered with jewels

The new Princess was showered with wonderful jewels at the time of her wedding – personal gifts from her new husband, grand jewels from the royal vaults from the Queen and the Queen Mother, plus magnificent wedding presents from heads of State.

However, many of the jewels were rather too grand and formal for the young Princess's taste. Traditionally, royal brides have been able to have their inherited jewels reset to suit current fashion and their own taste. Unfortunately for Diana, it is a practice that the Queen has rather frowned upon, regarding her inheritance as of historical rather than decorative value.

Undeterred, Diana has found inventive new ways to show off her jewels. In Australia, she wore an emerald necklace that belonged to Queen Mary as a headband when it was discovered that her tiara had inadvertently been left behind. On another occasion, she slipped a black velvet choker under the dazzling diamond necklace that was part of her wedding gift from the Crown Prince of Saudi Arabia. Yet another time, she pinned a huge sapphire brooch as large as a duck's egg and surrounded by diamonds, which had been given to her by the Queen Mother, onto a pearl choker. She has also been known to wear a rope of fake pearls down her back when dressed in a low-backed evening gown.

The Princess also has special dresses made to show off her gems. There was the midnight velvet dress collared with lace from Queen Victoria's Balmoral collection, which was designed to set off her sapphires.

And there was the dazzling blue gown made by the London-based Japanese designer Yuki which she wore for her audience with the late Emperor Hirohito; it set off beautifully the headband she'd had made from a diamond watchstrap, its clock-face replaced with a huge sapphire. She loved the overall effect so much that she kept it all on until she boarded her plane, much to the designer's delight – he saw it all on television.

An aura of mystery

A certain aura of mystery surrounds the fabulous diamond-and-pearl tiara that the Queen gave her new daughter-in-law on the occasion of her marriage. The tiara, with its diamond lovers' knots and nineteen pearl teardrops, originally belonged to Queen Mary. She reportedly had had it made by Garrard in 1914 using

pearls she had been given as a wedding present. However, its design owes more to kokoshnik tiaras made for the Romanov royal family, to whom Queen Mary was related. A very similar tiara was part of the cache discovered by the Bolsheviks in 1925.

More mystery has surrounded the fabulous emerald necklace given by the Queen to Princess Diana. A chunky choker-style with diamond-set cabochon emeralds interspersed with geometric plaques of diamonds with emerald centres in Art Deco style, it too originally belonged to the Queen's grandmother Queen Mary.

But was it, some wondered, part of the Alexandra emeralds reset for Wallis Simpson in the Thirties? It would not have been impossible for the Duchess of Windsor to give it to Prince Charles for his future bride so that the jewels could remain in the royal family.

The gossip proved to be unfounded, however, for photographs quite clearly show Queen Mary wearing this very same necklace as late as 1948, cleverly mixed in with her favourite pearls.

The Queen also gave Diana her personal gift of the Royal Family Order. The most exclusive of all the awards the monarch is able to confer, it consists of a miniature portrait of the Queen, ringed with diamonds, which Diana wears pinned to her evening dresses.

Gifts from the Gulf

Among the Princess's glittering wedding gifts was an opulent set of jewels from the Crown Prince of Saudi Arabia. A huge sapphire surrounded by a diamond sunburst and designed as a pendant, with matching earrings, was presented in a marble-green malachite box. It was embossed in gold with a palm tree and crossed-swords motif and a gold camel brooch.

Other gifts of jewels included a pearl set of

The Princess may own one of the world's most glittering collections of jewels, but she never feels restrained by tradition. On a visit to Australia, when she discovered her tiara had been left behind, she cleverly adapted a stunning emerald and diamond necklace. The Art Deco necklace, which had originally belonged to Queen Mary, had been given to Diana by the Queen.

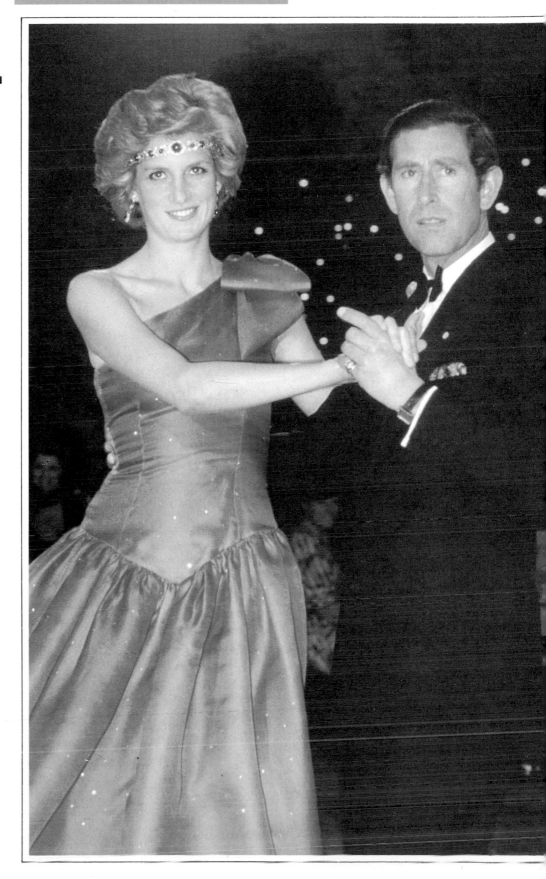

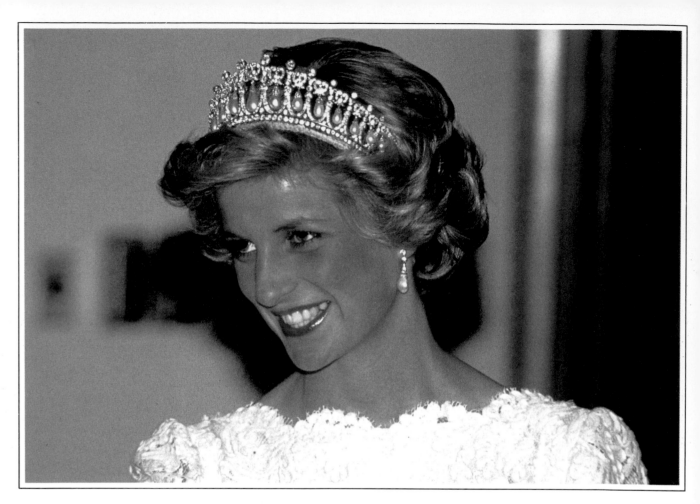

The Queen gave the Princess this fabulous tiara, with its diamond lover's knots and pearl teardrops, on the occasion of Diana's marriage. It originally belonged to Queen Mary.

watch, rings and cufflinks from the Emir of Qatar; a diamond watch from the United Arab Emirates; and an antique Indian necklace of gold choker with pearl fringe and multi-coloured gems including a central emerald, turquoises and diamonds, from the Crown Prince and Princess of Jordan.

Prince Charles's gifts

Yet more jewels were showered on the future Queen by her new husband, many of which were especially commissioned by him. There was the delicate white and yellow gold necklace of sapphire flowers and central motif of Prince of Wales feathers pendant designed by young jeweller Lexi Dick; a necklet of slate grey and cream baroque pearls by Leo de Vroomen; Wendy Ramshaw's feathered gold pin; some pieces by David Thomas; and a solid gold powder compact.

Most of Prince Charles's gifts to his bride were deeply romantic and personal and meant to be worn privately. The Prince and Princess take care to draw a strong dividing line between her public jewels and her personal jewels.

For example, Prince Charles gave her a gold charm bracelet at the time of their wedding, and in the tradition of Queen Victoria's consort Prince Albert, he adds charms to it for birthdays or special events. A solid-gold koala marks the couple's first joint visit to Australia, and in Canada Prince Charles gave Diana a wombat for her birthday.

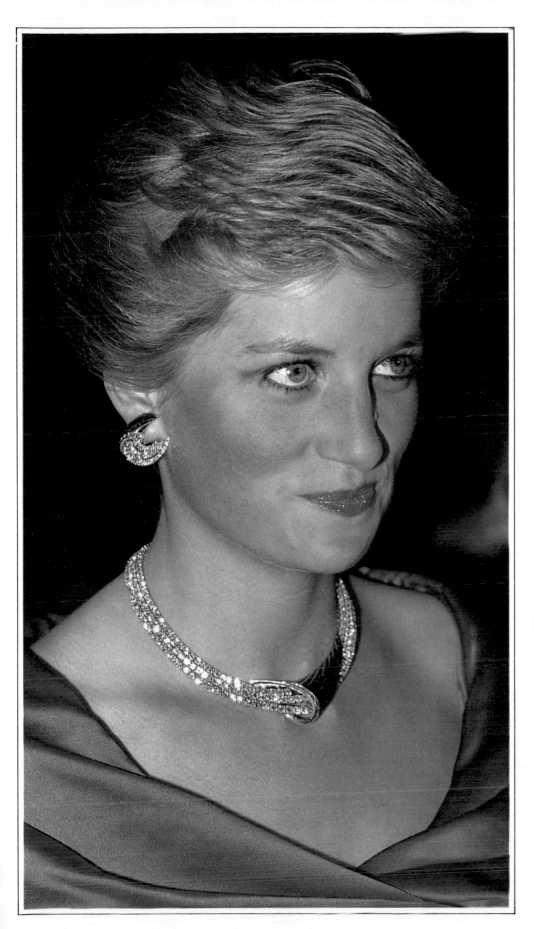

This modern-day
Princess does not rely
solely on royal heirlooms.
She also owns some
strong and important
contemporary pieces.
Here she wears a modern
sculptural necklace of
diamonds and sapphires,
with matching crescent
earrings. The set, which
also includes a bracelet,
was a gift from the Sultan
of Oman.

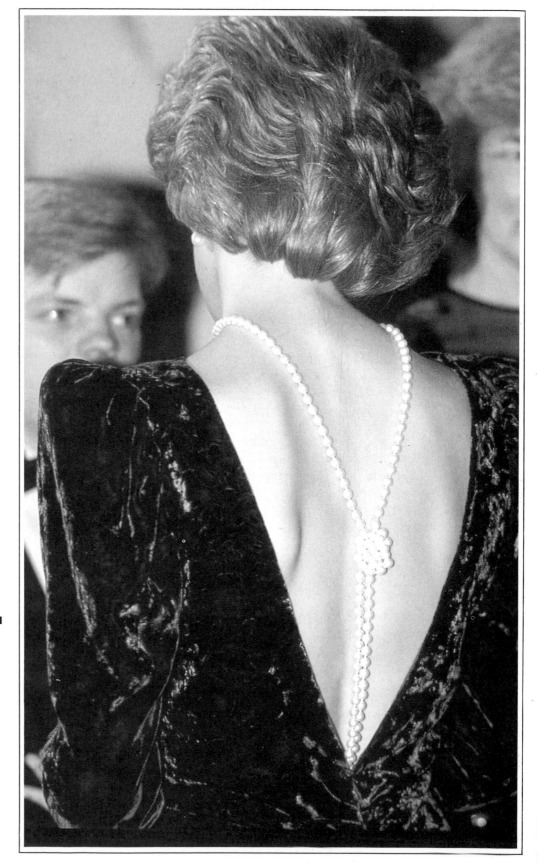

Another example of the Princess's stylish way of wearing jewellery. A simple but extra-long rope of pearls is worn with a knot at the back to play up a sensuous expanse of skin revealed by her low-backed evening dress.

But while most of Prince Charles's presents to his wife have been especially designed to his instructions, the magnificent sapphire-and-diamond engagement ring from Garrard, the Crown jewellers, was bought ready-made from a choice of eight rings brought to Balmoral. It even appeared in their catalogue priced at £28,000 ($51,300). Prince Charles's main wedding present to Diana was an important emerald-and-diamond antique bracelet bought from a jeweller who had been recommended by the Queen Mother.

A penchant for pearls

While sapphires to match her eyes are the obvious choice for the Princess, her personal penchant is for the pearls she has made so fashionable. Millions of copies were sold of her multi-stranded pearl choker with its central clasp and pearl drop, which she wore to go away for her honeymoon. She has a favourite seven-strand pearl choker with a diamond clasp, and others with opal or turquoise clasps, as well as single-strand pearl necklaces.

However grand the occasion, the Princess will often settle for pearls rather than diamonds. And like most fashionable young women, she is seldom seen without earrings even when she is wearing jeans. She would prefer to leave off her make-up than her earrings.

The psychology of earrings

According to Professor Ray Bull, Head of Psychology at Southampton University, many women don't feel themselves without their earrings. "To get on in the world, women create an image for themselves – with clothes and accessories – that they feel projects an aura of glamour, or accomplishment or status. Take away the earrings and you're chipping away at the vital self-image," he asserts.

Diana's current favourite pearl earrings are

> ### THE GOLDEN RULES OF JEWELLERY WEARING
> **1** You can't have too many pairs of earrings – they frame your face flatteringly and are easy-to-wear with anything.
> **2** Don't be afraid to wear glitzy jewellery with casual clothes, and vice versa – it's the surprise of the unexpected that makes for chic.
> **3** Mix pieces together; a gilt necklace can be worn with a pearl one, and several brooches on one lapel can make an interesting focal point to a simple outfit.
> **4** Follow Princess Diana's lead and wear necklaces in new ways. For instance, she twists pearl ropes into bracelets, and has worn an emerald necklace as a headband.

the fashionable but inexpensive Venus faux-pearl drops sold at the New York Metropolitan Museum of Art shop and also available by mail order from them. A copy of the earrings in the famous Rubens painting, "Venus before the Mirror", they are usually sold as worn in the painting, with one black pearl and one creamy pearl drop, but the Princess prefers to wear them as a matched set in cream.

Rhinestones in public

Ironically, the Princess of Wales is just as happy with her faux-pearl drop earrings or snake brooch as she is with her grandest jewels. The whole perception of jewellery has moved on a long way in recent years since the time when costume jewellery was merely a pale imitation of the real thing.

As Simon Butler of Butler & Wilson says, "Any stigma that there may have been about wearing imitation jewellery has been demolished by the Princess of Wales, who is perfectly happy to wear her rhinestones for public engagements."

5
Gilt-edged Shopping

*G*one are the days when the royal family rarely entered a shop. Diana, who used to shop without a care in her pre-royal days, continues to shop more or less as she pleases. She thinks nothing of strolling down her local high street and popping into chain stores like everyone else – but luxury lingerie is usually tried on in the privacy of Kensington Palace.

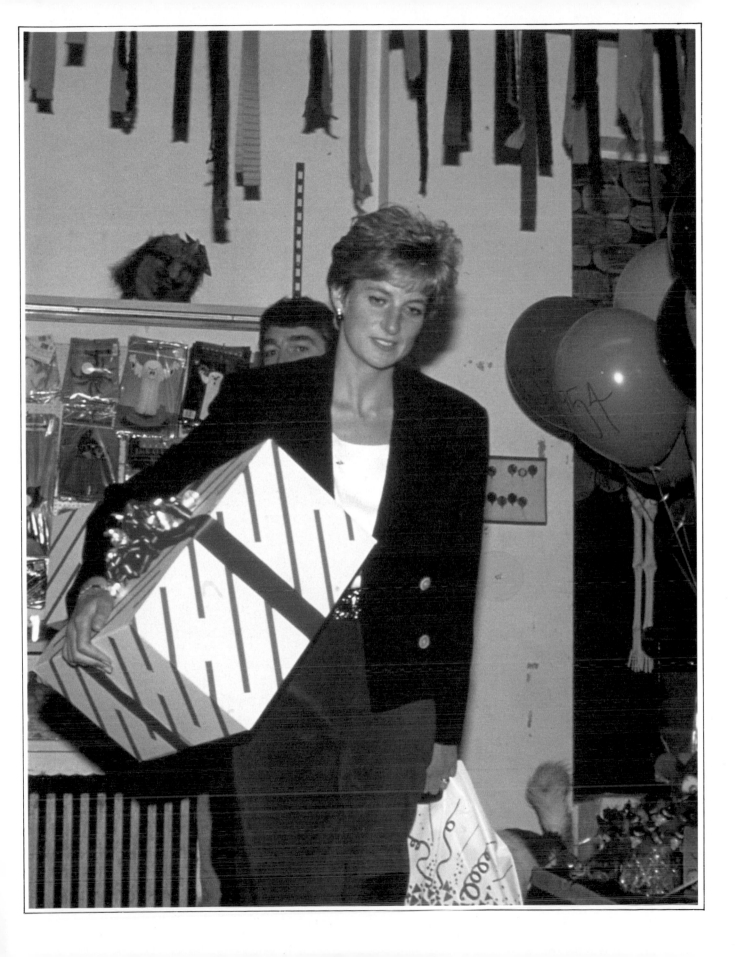

While it is rare to see the Queen or other senior members of the royal family dropping casually into the shops, the young royals, accustomed as they were to shop as they pleased in their formative years, continue to do so. (There will, however, usually be a discreet detective in attendance and perhaps a lady-in-waiting or friend as well.)

Before her marriage, Lady Diana Spencer, as she then was, had freedom to do as she pleased. Diana loved to drop into shops like Laura Ashley and Harvey Nichols after she had finished at the kindergarten in London's Pimlico where she taught.

Kensington Di Street

Diana enjoys shopping in her local high street just like any woman. Hers simply happens to be Kensington High Street, which is just down the road from Kensington Palace. It has now been nicknamed by many as Kensington Di Street owing to the frequency with which Diana is spotted there.

Here she will nip into the downstairs food department of Marks & Spencer for her favourite salt-and-vinegar crisps and pop into the Body Shop to stock up on beauty products. She will drop into Benetton for casual clothes for Prince William and Prince Harry, buying two of everything to avoid squabbles.

Often, casually dressed in jeans and sweater like any other young mother after dropping the boys off at school, she goes totally unrecognized.

Knightsbridge is a more sophisticated haunt where she may fit in some morning shopping before lunching with a girl friend at San Lorenzo, the fashionable Italian restaurant.

Society's favourite store

The Princess quite often shops at Harrods, probably the world's most prestigious store,

and holder of no less than four royal warrants: those of Prince Charles, the Queen, the Queen Mother and the Duke of Edinburgh.

Sometimes she is in there as often as twice a week, but she usually arranges to go at 10.00 am when the store opens and is at its quietest. She slips in through door number ten at the back where the parking is easier.

Very often the Princess will ask her lady-in-waiting to ring in advance to warn Harrods to expect her. She is personally looked after by Brian Ames, Director of Customer Services, who looks after all visiting royalty and VIPs. Sometimes Brian and the Princess will wander through the store together; or, if he has had advance warning of what she is looking for, he will gather a selection of the items together in advance and have everything waiting for her in a private suite.

While the whole of the royal family tend to regard Harrods as their corner store, the staff are super-discreet and go out of their way to protect their illustrious clients.

The executive service is also available to busy Harrods' account customers, as well as visiting dignitaries and their wives – Raisa Gorbachev is one who has used it to try things on in private. "We're here to serve people and make things easier for them", says the store's Media Director Michael Cole.

In the luxurious marble-floored cosmetics hall on the ground floor, Diana may buy items from the American Erno Laszlo skin care system. And also on the ground floor, she will stop off in the accessories department for tights and stockings by Christian Dior and Le Bourget. Sometimes she asks to see ideas for wedding and christening presents.

Diana likes to shop for underwear at Harrods too. She is particularly partial to expensive designer lingerie from the Italian La Perla label – she has several items from their Fortuny-style pleated range in white, black and peach. She also buys Derek Roe's men's pyjamas.

High chic at Harvey Nichols

Not far from Harrods is Harvey Nichols, which is famous for being Diana's favourite shop. Here she is more likely to pop in unannounced just as she used to when she was a kindergarten teacher. The difference is that now she will normally dash in by a side entrance, leaving her car on a double yellow line, with her detective not far behind.

Harvey Nichols is unique, in that it appeals as much to the young Sloanes as it does to their grandmothers. Originally best known as the place where the dowagers held their accounts, it has become in recent years the most fashionable store in London, and a showcase for the very best in international design.

Here, on its compact six floors with its pleasant ambience, Diana can find a superb selection of designer clothes and accessories, plus the cream of cosmetics and perfumes. Here, too, she has the use of a private suite, where things can be gathered together in advance for her selection and where she can try clothes on in privacy.

On the ground floor, she buys her favourite Annick Goutal Passion perfume with its fragrant matching pebbles to scent her rooms. She purchases cosmetics from Clinique and Dior, stocks up on Donna Karan silky nude-toned tights from America and browses through the newest arrivals of designer jewellery and accessories.

On the first floor there are showcases for the international labels that she likes to wear in private. In just a few minutes she can get an instant view of the latest looks from all the major fashion capitals. There are entire shops for designers like Ralph Lauren, Donna Karan and Isaac Mizrahi from New York; and Sonia Rykiel, Claude Montana and Jean Paul Gaultier from Paris; plus there are spacious areas for the Italian designers Dolce & Gabbana and Moschino.

It was from Harvey Nichols that the Princess ordered the stunning red-and-black checked Moschino suit she wore to Princess Eugenie's christening. The store showed her the collection in advance in album form and she herself chose to mix the red-and-white jacket with the black-and-white skirt. The zany and talented designer was thrilled with the idea – it's exactly the way he likes to see his clothes worn.

On the second floor, Diana browses through the less expensive and more casual secondary ranges of top label designers – like Donna Karan's cheaper DKNY label. And on the third floor she hunts down sportswear.

On the fourth floor, furnishings, Diana likes to look at the stylish fashion-orientated room sets by fashion labels like Ralph Lauren and Mulberry – both very country-house style. She would love to decorate her rooms at Balmoral with some of Ralph Lauren's amusing tartan furnishings and furniture.

In the old days, Diana would often head on up to the fifth floor of Harvey Nichols for coffee or lunch at their pleasantly informal restaurant, Harveys. But in recent years, she has become very partial to lunching with girl friends at Le Caprice in Arlington Street, just off Piccadilly. Sitting at a corner window table, she often orders their Eggs Benedict or salmon fishcakes with sorrel sauce, preceded by a Caesar Salad or their famous Bang Bang Chicken.

Beauchamp Place: a favourite haunt

Alternatively, she might head off down to Beauchamp Place, which has been a favourite haunt since the days when she dressed at Bruce Oldfield and Caroline Charles.

She might drop into Janet Reger's lingerie

boutique, where she will choose luxurious silk and satin underwear in black or white. She has had bras, briefs, camiknickers and slips from here and has recently bought their satin "teddies" – bodysuits cut flatteringly on the bias.

Usually she will take the items to try on in the privacy of the Palace or ring up to have things sent round if she's very busy. "She treats the girls in the shop with such respect and knows all their names," says Janet Reger. "And sometimes we will make things especially for her if they're not in stock in the shop. But they are always styles from the current range."

Almost next door to Janet Reger is the boutique owned by Lady Tryon and called Kanga, which is Prince Charles's pet name for the vivacious and bubbly Australian. Initially, the Princess was wary of Charles's female confidants, but later she was spotted lunching with Lady Tryon at San Lorenzo. She has worn several of her usefully non-crush printed rayon dresses to watch polo or attend Wimbledon.

Fashionable Fulham Road

The now fashionable Fulham Road is another favourite shopping area for Princess Diana. It is handy for when she is visiting designer Catherine Walker at her shop in Sydney Street, which runs off it.

As well as her frequent stops at Butler & Wilson (see page 50), she has spotted items in the window of Tatters just across the road and ordered one of their elaborately beaded short evening dresses. Best known for wonderful antique-style wedding dresses in lace and satin, the American owner Missie Graves has recently added a range of sophisticated short dresses with intricate beaded embroidery.

Diana also buys lightweight padded shoulder bags and matching purses in colourful Provençal prints from Souleiado, the Tarascon-based family firm with a branch in the Fulham Road. While she doesn't normally like shoulder bags because they spoil her silhouette, these are as light as a feather and perfect for casual occasions such as polo.

Next to Tatters is Night Owls, the sleepwear specialists where Diana buys nightdresses and pyjamas. In fact, this area of London is like a tiny fashion village for the Princess. It also has the great advantage over Knightsbridge in that there are no crowds or crush; even the parking does not pose too much of a problem.

Sources of patterned sweaters

Among the many fashion trends that the Princess of Wales has set was that for boldly patterned sweaters. She loves to wear these for the casual side of her life, teaming them with jeans tucked into boots and a jaunty baseball cap on her head.

Her original cloud-and-sky patterned jumpers came from Inca, the Peruvian crafts shop in Elizabeth Street, in London's Belgravia. The famous sheep sweaters were by Warm and Wonderful, who are now renamed Muir & Osborne and have moved from Kensington to Primrose Hill.

She has also been seen at a branch of Jumpers in the country town of Cirencester, which is conveniently near the Wales' country home Highgrove. Here she bought two cotton sweaters: one in navy cotton with a pattern of brightly coloured elephants, and another in cream with multi-coloured flowers.

When she's weekending at Highgrove with her family, the Princess enjoys shopping in her local market town of Cirencester dressed casually like any other young mother.

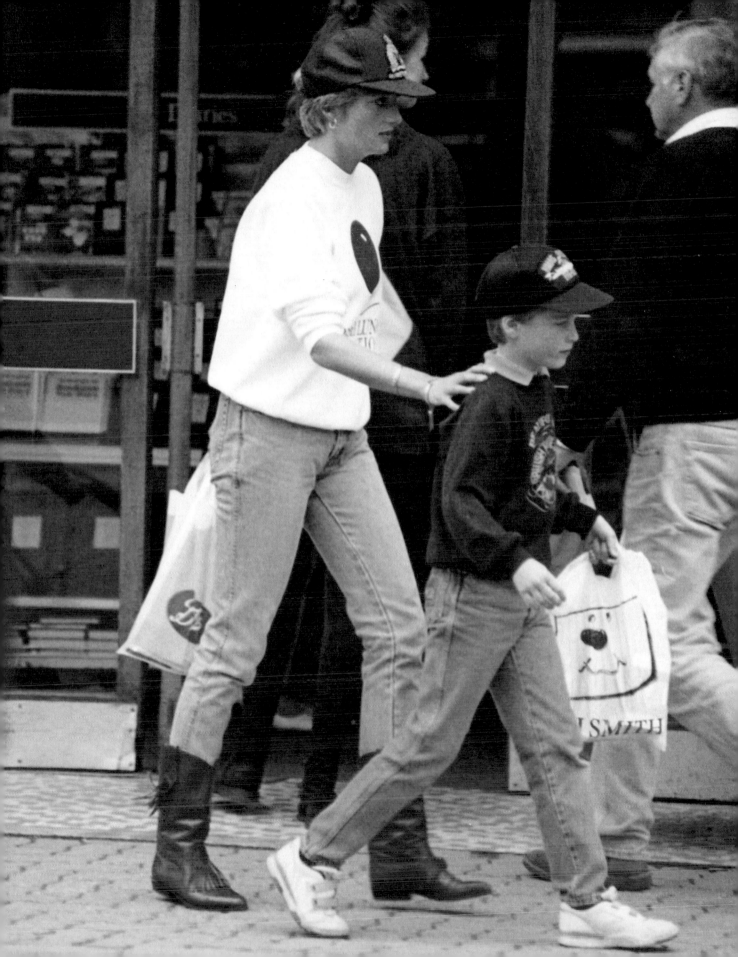

Shopping for shoes

For years, Diana would buy all her shoes at Charles Jourdan, the top French shoe designers whose London branch is in Brompton Road, close to Harrods. She or her lady-in-waiting would telephone in advance to make an appointment, and then she would choose shoes and matching handbags in the privacy of an upstairs room. The styles would be from the regular range but were made in special colours to go with the clothes for her royal tours.

"It was a great boost for the firm and very exciting for all the staff when we saw our shoes in pictures, and in fact she still uses many of her old handbags," says ex-Jourdan managing director, John Gairdner. A charming Scotsman whose two uncles were equerries to George VI, he would personally fit the princess's feet and was jokingly known as the royal footman. "She has fabulous feet," he says. "It's a very intimate and personal thing fitting feet."

But when John Gairdner left, so did the Princess, choosing to have her shoes made instead by Rayne, the Queen's cobblers. Her favourite shoe at Jourdan had been an elegant pump with a little shaped heel that looked higher than it actually was, and Rayne copied the Jourdan last for her.

Originally, the Princess was very self-conscious about her height and didn't want to tower above her husband, as she's already 2.5 cm (1 inch) taller without heels. But now that she is much more self-confident, she sees her 1.79 m (5 feet 10½ inches) as a fashion bonus and will happily wear much higher heels, such as those from Manolo Blahnik in Old Church Street, Chelsea, where celebrities like Bianca Jagger and Paloma Picasso shop for shoes.

Exclusive Mayfair

Cheaper, spur-of-the-moment shoe buys might well come from Pied à Terre in Sloane Street or South Molton Street. South Molton Street is a little shopping street closed to cars but full of high-fashion boutiques; it runs between crowded Oxford Street and exclusive Brook Street, in London's Mayfair.

In South Molton Street, Diana also likes to see what's new at the Browns boutiques. They stock high fashion from the best international designers, such as Donna Karan from New York; Genny, Romeo Gigli and Dolce & Gabbana from Italy; and Sonia Rykiel, Azzedine Alaïa and Claude Montana from France.

The store is actually made up of several small shops on three floors which are all linked together. It has an intimate atmosphere, a soft and sophisticated ambience and staff who are discretion itself. The stylish owner Joan Burnstein has carefully trained them to advise customers on how to wear their clothes and how to mix the season's new buy with existing clothes.

This is the place were Madonna will drop in to pick up a psychedelic print dress by Pucci or a rhinestoned bodysuit by Dolce & Gabbana. Unfortunately, the Princess cannot be so adventurous. "Sometimes I can be a little outrageous, which is quite nice. But only sometimes," she has been quoted as saying. She is more likely to choose a beautifully made suit from Moschino's couture range, like the bottle-green one with gilt buttons that she wore for the State visit of the Italian president.

Fenwick of Bond Street

Diana is also a fan of Fenwick, the fashionable Bond Street department store that excels at accessories and inexpensive high fashion for working girls. However, she does not pop in there in the way that she used to; instead, the store sends things around to the Palace for her approval, including bundles of the bras she likes to buy from there.

Alternatively, Anna Harvey, of British

Vogue, unofficially helps Diana still and will arrange for things to be sent to her, like the hot-pink gaberdine suit by Irish designer Paul Costelloe that Diana bought from Fenwick last year. "She used to dive in through the front door for toiletries and tights," says a spokeswoman, "but we've not seen her for a while."

The bras that Diana buys from Fenwick are the Gossard Glossies – very sheer, slightly sparkly styles without seams or fussy detailing, which give her a smooth, sleek line under sheer shirts, clingy sweaters and sports clothes. Far from being elitist, they're exactly what any girl would wear, and she buys the matching bikini briefs too, all in white or a nude-toned skin colour.

But Fenwick's ground-floor accessories and cosmetics department is still very much the place to find the less-pressured young royals like Lady Helen Windsor and Lady Sarah Armstrong-Jones. Unfettered by the demands of public life, they can still shop there for the casual clothes they prefer.

Choosing clothes for Prince Charles

Prince Charles has rarely been seen inside a shop of any sort, so in order to carve out his new, much more modern image, Diana has had to undertake his shopping as well as hers.

She has weaned him away from his "young-fogey" image by changing his tailors to Anderson & Shepherd in Savile Row. They make him classic double-breasted pin-striped suits with narrow lapels and trousers with cuffs.

The Princess has collected for her husband an array of colourful silk ties which, however, he is seldom seen wearing, preferring to stick to the safety of navy and red spots.

Mail-order shopping

As a busy working mother with never enough time to fit in everything she would like to

SLOANE RANGER LAND

The "Sloane Ranger" set, which Princess Diana has always been very much part of, are so-called because of their strong affinity with London's Sloane Square and Sloane Street, which runs between Sloane Square and Knightsbridge. Every newly engaged Sloane Ranger – and Diana was no exception – has her wedding list at the department store Peter Jones in Sloane Square or at the General Trading Company, just around the corner in Sloane Street. Diana still shops for presents at the General Trading Company, which sells up-market items for the home ranging from boot-scrapers to fine china dinner services.

Just opposite is the chemist's shop where she has for years bought her supply of energy-giving royal jelly.

In fact, Diana, like all good Sloane Rangers, was shopping in the area long before her marriage. As a young kindergarten teacher, she bought pretty, frilled, Victorian-style blouses, lightweight floral-print skirts and velvet knickerbockers from the Laura Ashley shop in Harriet Street, just off Sloane Street.

In between the General Trading Company at the south end of Sloane Street and Harvey Nichols at the north end, where Sloane Street meets Knightsbridge, there are many of Diana's favourite stopping-off points.

At Browns, the Princess likes to look at the cream of the latest designer labels, especially Moschino. No doubt she will also be popping in to London's first Christian Lacroix shop virtually next door to Browns. Chanel, Valentino and Karl Lagerfeld are all designers Diana admires and whose clothes she likes to wear privately, and all have shops in Sloane Street.

Princess Diana will be unlikely to resist a peek into the tempting new Gucci shop. Its stylish design director Dawn Mello is making the classic Italian label even more of a cult for Sloane Rangers, who especially love the soft suede loafers and fashionable silk squares.

accomplish, Princess Diana also indulges in the comfort of armchair shopping, ordering quite a lot of her clothes, including swimwear and thermal underwear, from mail-order catalogues. Worries over security mean that this is an increasingly popular way for the royals to shop.

All the royals order from the glossy magazine-style Christmas catalogues produced by stores like Harrods, Fortnum & Mason, Simpsons, Harvey Nichols and Hamleys, all of which

sport royal warrants. Secretaries or ladies-in-waiting telephone their orders and also visit shops as "scouts", arranging to have goods sent on approval.

Designer thermals

It is by mail order that Diana buys her by-now-famous thermal underwear. She orders like anyone else from the catalogue produced by the Damart company, who now have updated their image with a designer range by top lingerie specialist Juliet Dunn.

This new range is far more fashionable and streamlined, with second-skin bodysuits in Thermolactyl, Damart's exclusive fibre which retains body heat while repelling moisture. In this fibre there are pretty lacy cami-briefs, either sleeveless or with cap or long sleeves.

Juliet has also mixed Thermolactyl with silk for cami-briefs and camisoles. There is even one cosy bodysuit with detachable feathered collar and cuffs that makes it adaptable for disco wear, but so far the Princess has not been seen in one.

Princess Diana orders German clothes from the ultra-glossy, ultra-thick, magazine-style brochures featuring her favourite supermodels; they are put out by manufacturers Escada, Laurel and Mondi. From Mondi, she has bought amusing coordinated separates like a spotted red-and-white sweater with matching socks. It was from the Escada catalogue that she ordered the cosy yellow-and-black coat that she wore for a visit to Germany.

Mail-order swimwear

Princess Diana also finds mail order a convenient way to order her swimwear, such as the striking Gottex set in ocelot print that she wore on holiday on the island of Necker, and the stunning geometric print bikini by the American Jantzen swimwear company.

PRINCESS DIANA'S COMPREHENSIVE SHOPPING GUIDE

KENSINGTON HIGH STREET
Benetton for boys' clothes
The Body Shop for beauty products

KNIGHTSBRIDGE
Harrods for underwear and wedding presents
Harvey Nichols for international designer clothes, perfume and tights
Janet Reger in Beauchamp Place for silk undies and lingerie
Kanga in Beauchamp Place for printed dresses

FULHAM ROAD
Butler & Wilson for fun jewellery
Souleiado for Provençal-print handbags
Tatters for beaded evening dresses
Night Owls for pyjamas and dressing gowns

MAYFAIR
Browns in South Molton Street for designer clothes
Pied à Terre in South Molton Street for high-fashion shoes
Fenwick in Bond Street for underwear and Paul Costelloe suits

MAIL-ORDER SHOPPING
Damart thermal underwear
Escada, Laurel and Mondi
Gottex and Jantzen swimwear
Harrods
Harvey Nichols
Simpsons

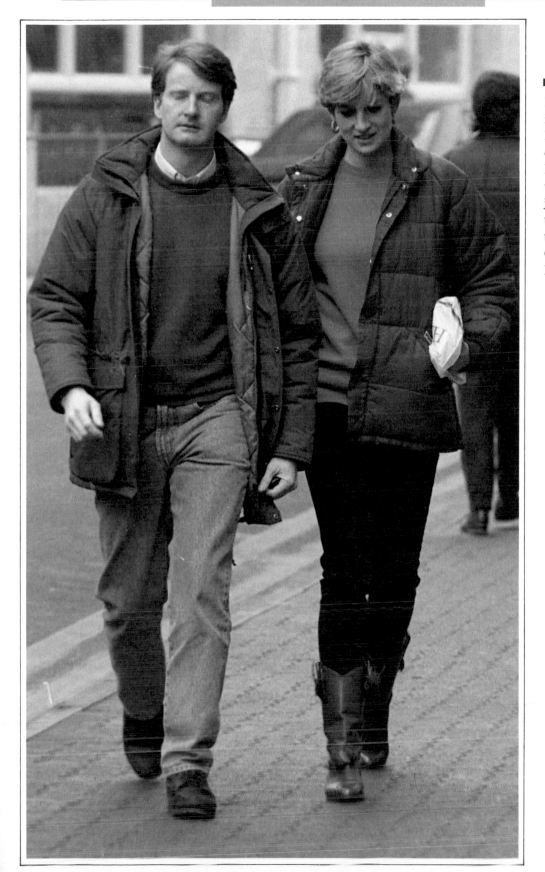

Even when she's buried in the country, the Princess of Wales – here clad in the traditional English country weekend uniform of Puffa jacket, jeans and boots – escapes to the delights of country-town shopping in Cirencester, near her Highgrove home.

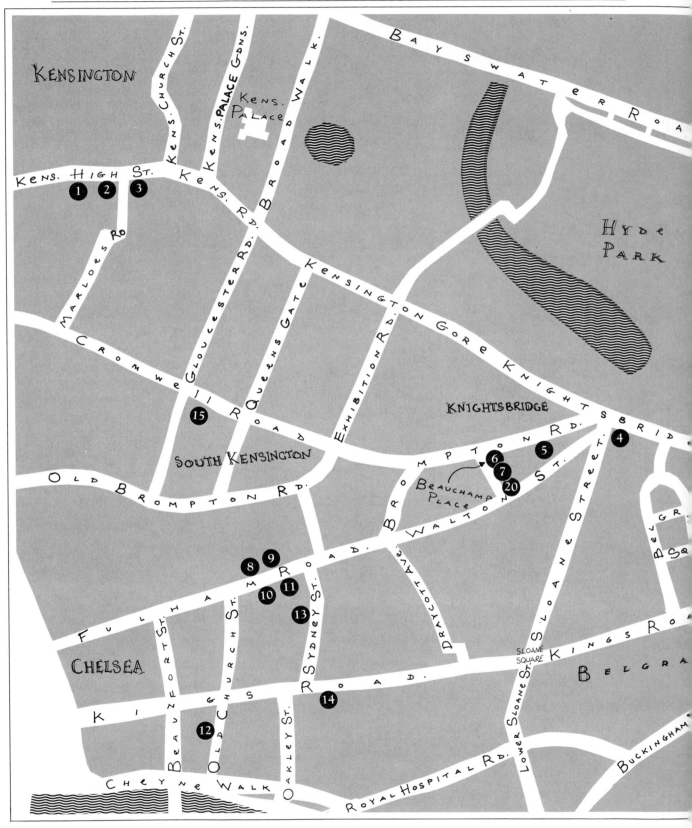

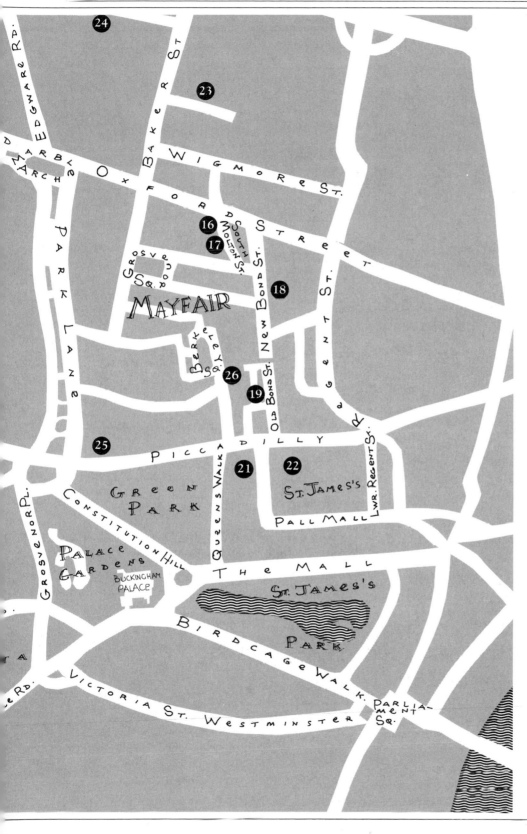

ROYAL LONDON

The map shows London fashion shops, restaurants, beauty salons and hairdressers which are favourites of the Princess of Wales.

FASHION
1 The Body Shop
2 Benetton
3 Marks & Spencer
4 Harvey Nichols
5 Harrods
6 Janet Reger
7 Kanga
8 Night Owls
9 Tatters
10 Souleiado
11 Butler & Wilson
12 Manolo Blahnik
13 Catherine Walker
14 Edina Ronay
15 Victor Edelstein
16 Browns
17 Pied à Terre
18 Fenwick
19 Chanel

RESTAURANTS
20 San Lorenzo
21 Le Caprice
22 Green's

BEAUTY
23 Daniel Galvin
24 Janet Filderman
25 Danièle Ryman at the Park Lane Hotel
26 Temple McAdam

6

Shedding Excess with Success

*A*s everyone who has ever tried knows, losing weight is difficult – and keeping it off is even harder. But there is no doubt that Princess Diana has won her battle with the scales. After trying various crash diets she has discovered that sensible, healthy eating is the long-term solution. And she manages to maintain her enviable figure despite a continuous succession of official and social functions involving food.

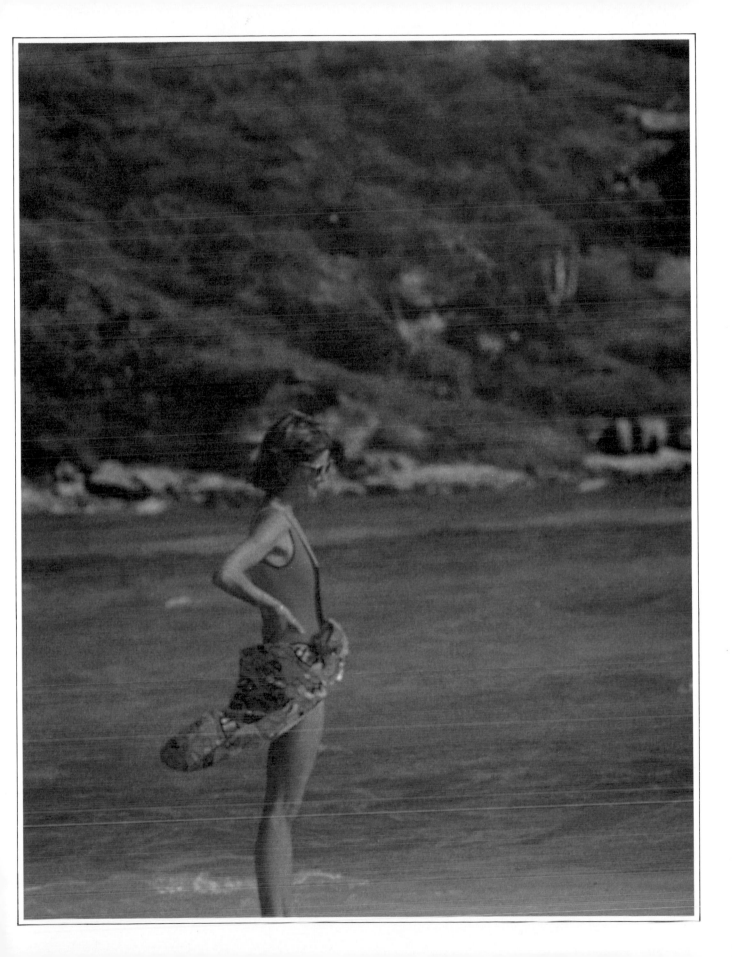

They say the camera never lies. It does, of course – it enlarges horribly, something that most much-photographed women soon discover. That is why it's often a shock to meet a celebrity in the flesh and discover a much slighter, slimmer person than you had imagined. It is also the reason television presenters and film stars are continually on diets.

This tendency was all too obvious to the Princess of Wales when she first joined the House of Windsor and became the most photographed woman in the world.

Less is more

At the time of her engagement, Diana was a pretty but slightly plump nineteen-year-old with a penchant for chocolate bars. Today, the model-slim Princess is trim and glowing with health. Her designer clothes, in size 10 (US size 8) look terrific. And she has managed to achieve this despite the continual round of official luncheons, cocktail receptions, gargantuan banquets, not forgetting the private lunches and dinner parties she enjoys.

Her sensational transformation has not happened overnight. She has worked exceptionally hard at remodelling her figure, both during pregnancy and after the birth of her children. Just how did she do it?

Losing weight for the wedding

As a pretty but slightly plump nineteen-year-old kindergarten teacher who had just captured her prince, Diana hated that first official picture of her. Flaunting her huge new sapphire engagement ring, she was wearing a rather shapeless matching blue Cojana suit that had been hurriedly bought off the peg. It actually made her look plumper than she was – and it made her determined to slim down for her fairytale wedding.

Like many brides-to-be, she put herself on a stringent diet to shed weight quickly in the fairly short run-up to the wedding. Suddenly, she was shunning the chips (French fries) and the chocolates that she loves and sticking to a far healthier regime of chicken or fish with lots of fresh fruit and vegetables. And like many other brides-to-be she didn't find it too difficult – there was so much to plan and do that she barely had time to eat.

The stress and strain of not only planning a huge wedding but becoming royal helped the weight drop off. By the time of her wedding she had lost about 3 kg (7 pounds) – her plump cheeks had fined down and her whittled waistline showed off the crinoline skirt of her Emanuel wedding gown to its full glory. She looked every bit the fairytale princess.

The effects of motherhood

Soon after, the Princess became pregnant with William and was concentrating on getting through her pregnancy rather than watching her weight. She has admitted several times that pregnancy does not suit her and she felt ill much of the time.

Like most new mothers, Diana had imagined that she would be back to her old shape almost immediately after the birth. She was therefore mortified when she was pictured with Prince Charles and the new baby, Prince William, on the steps of the Lindo Wing of St Mary's Hospital still wearing a voluminous green maternity dress. It was the only thing she could cram her still-bulky figure into.

Immediately afterwards, the Princess disappeared from public life, immersing herself in motherhood and working hard at losing weight – as fast as she could.

Before her pregnancy, she had been beginning to enjoy her new wardrobe of designer clothes and her reputation as a fashion leader.

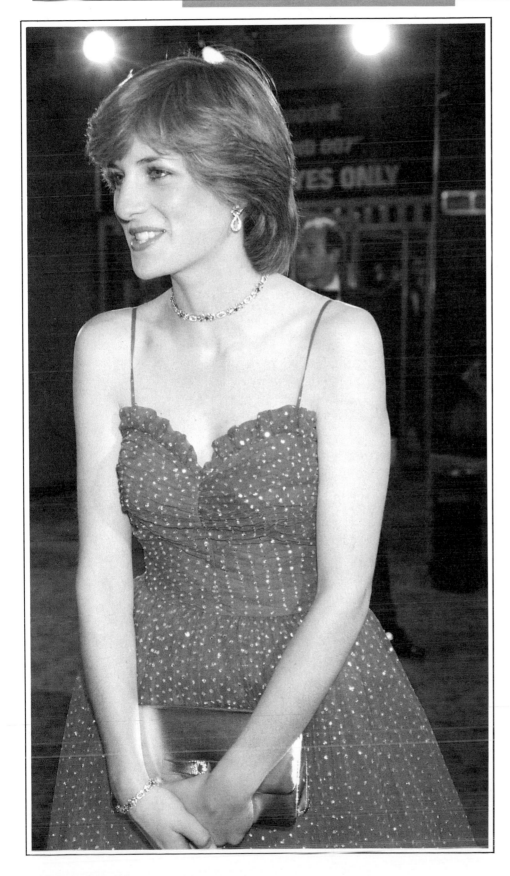

Diana learned quickly how much heavier the camera can make a person look. After the first photographs appeared in the press following her engagement, and also after the press photographs of her following Prince William's birth, she worked hard at losing weight. At the same time she educated herself in which styles are the most flattering, and which to avoid.

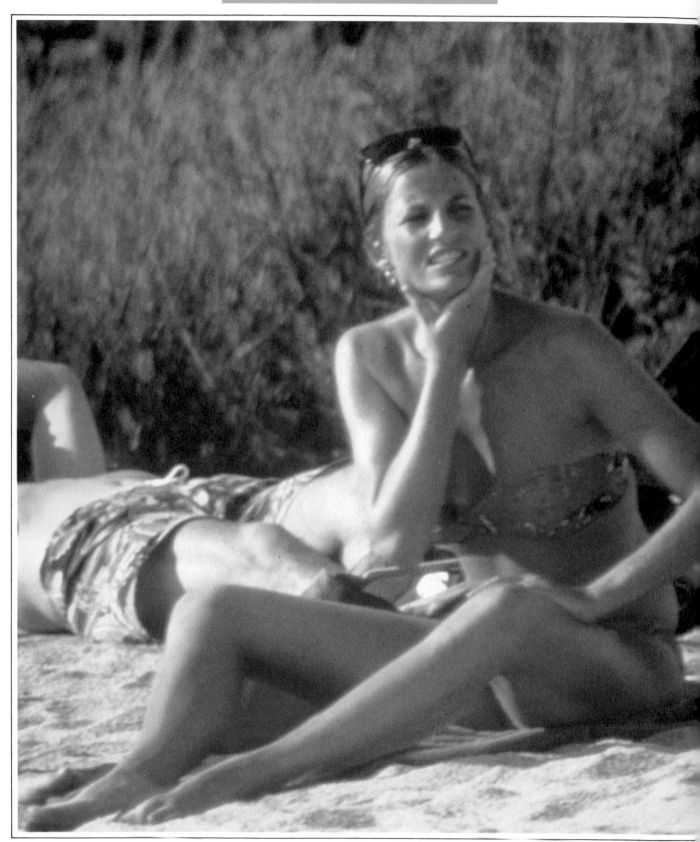

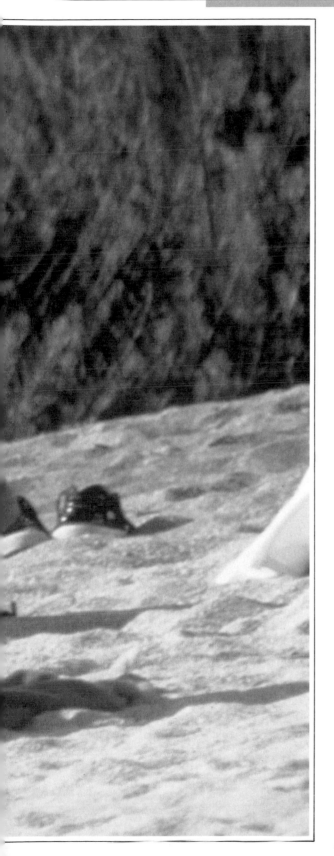

Now that she was no longer pregnant, she knew that the cameras of the world's press would be again focusing on her in minute detail, and she wanted to look her best.

A woman's metabolism changes after having her first baby, and looking after the new infant can drain the body's resources beyond belief. The diet that the Princess had followed so successfully before her marriage was too drastic for a new mother.

Accusations of anorexia

Diana soon became painfully thin, giving rise to fears of anorexia nervosa, an illness characterized by obsessive slimming. Diana's sister Sarah had already suffered from this.

A palace insider denied that the Princess was suffering from anorexia. "Any talk of anorexia is rubbish, total nonsense; a woman changes after having a baby," said the source.

But later there were worries that the pin-thin Princess was also serving as a slimline role model for girls as young as eight suffering from the eating disorder. "Many children remain convinced that beauty and success are due to being thin," child-health expert Rachel Waugh was quoted as saying.

Barbara Cartland, Princess Diana's step-grandmother, begged youngsters not to try to copy the Princess. "She is naturally slim. People should not try to be like her," she stressed. "People should eat normal food and take a lot of exercise and they will be all right."

In an effort to adjust to her demanding lifestyle, Diana adopted little tricks to prevent

Today, thanks to a careful diet, as well as a rigorous exercise routine, the tall, willowy Princess has a near-perfect figure, with the proportions of a model.

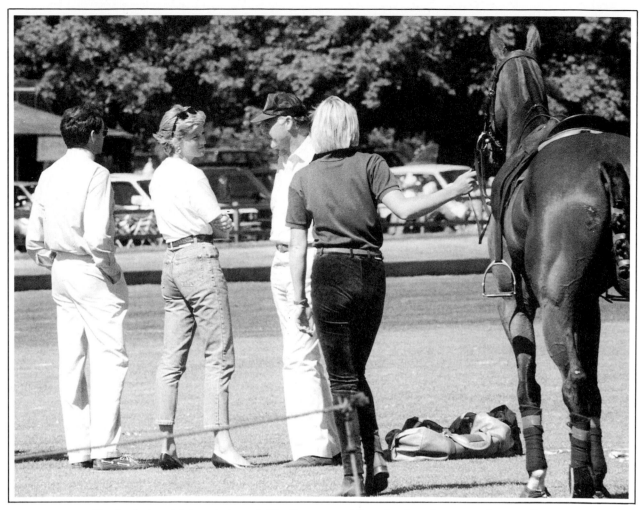

Slender but certainly not starved. Slimline cropped jeans by American manufacturer Guess
play up Diana's fabulous figure on the polo field.

herself from eating the wrong foods. For instance, so that she wouldn't overeat at a banquet, she would sometimes eat something light but filling in private beforehand – something she still does.

In addition, she has learned to push her food around on her plate instead of quickly polishing it all off. She hates to eat in public anyway and also dislikes eating when flying. All this was noted by onlookers and contributed enormously to the anorexia theory.

Healthier eating habits

The Princess had also totally changed the haphazard eating habits of her bachelor-girl days.

As a child she had developed a passion for shepherd's pie – a boarding-school special of minced beef and onions topped with mashed potato – as well as for baked beans and bread-and-butter pudding.

Similarly, when Diana shared a flat in London's Coleherne Court, just off the Old Brompton Road, she skipped breakfast and lived on chocolate bars (especially Mars, Kit Kat and Yorkie), sandwiches and spaghetti.

Once she married her prince, all this changed. A much more grown-up lifestyle, with a new husband to cater for, meant proper three-course meals once or twice a day. There were also all those banquets, dinners and lunches with the many courses. It was all too easy to pile on the weight.

Luckily, Prince Charles is himself extremely health-conscious and has influenced Diana's eating habits to a considerable extent. The wholesome "lifestyle-diet" which he and his family enjoy, coupled with vigorous exercise and Diana's tricks for avoiding rich, fattening food, have prevented all the multi-course meals from having much impact on her figure. Now she no longer has to diet drastically – her weight is stable.

Homegrown at Highgrove

The Prince and Princess avoid red meat like beef and pork, eating plenty of fish and chicken accompanied by lots of fresh vegetables (carrots, courgettes, cabbages, potatoes, peppers, turnips) that Charles grows in the garden at Highgrove.

Most of the time they avoid heavy food, privately preferring poached salmon from Balmoral, light egg dishes, salads and baked potatoes, with light fruit sorbets instead of heavy puddings. A passionate gardener, Charles even grows tomatoes on the roof garden at Kensington Palace.

They enjoy fresh pasta – ravioli, agnoletti, macaroni and spaghetti – which they eat with a light sauce as a main course, perhaps preceded by a fishy first course.

Neither Charles nor Diana drinks spirits. They serve a light German wine and champagne when they are entertaining, although the Princess generally prefers mineral water or fruit juice. She keeps bottles of sparkling mineral water at hand in both her living room and her bedroom at all times.

A typical lunch on a quiet day at home, at either Kensington Palace or Highgrove, will include a vegetable soup with organic ingredients from the garden. If there is no official dinner or engagement in the evening, Diana will plan the dinner menu with one of two cooks. Very often, there will be vegetable soup again, followed by poached salmon, new potatoes and fresh vegetables, and then fresh fruit, cheese and coffee.

Prince Charles is especially keen on organic food, refusing to have any meat in his home from animals reared with artificial stimulants. Diana prefers fish anyway.

Breakfast – a good investment

Princess Diana has learned the importance of eating a proper breakfast, rather than the quick cup of instant coffee that she would snatch before dashing off to the kindergarten in her pre-marriage days. Forgoing breakfast made her susceptible to cheese sandwiches and chocolate bars halfway through the morning and contributed to her puppy fat.

These days, the Princess realizes that breakfast is the most important meal of the day, boosting energy and enabling her to eat less for both lunch and dinner. After her early morning swim, she breakfasts on either home-made muesli with skimmed milk, or wholemeal toast thinly spread with butter and honey, or chocolate croissants. She also has a fizzy multivitamin tablet popped into a glass of mineral

ROYAL WAYS OF KEEPING TRIM
- Don't eat between meals.
- Substitute honey for sugar.
- Take herbal tea without milk or sugar instead of regular tea or coffee.
- Eat lots of fresh vegetables, salads and fruits – garden-fresh where possible.
- Don't eat when tired.
- Drink alcohol in moderation. Avoid sweet wines, sherries, liqueurs and sugary cocktails.

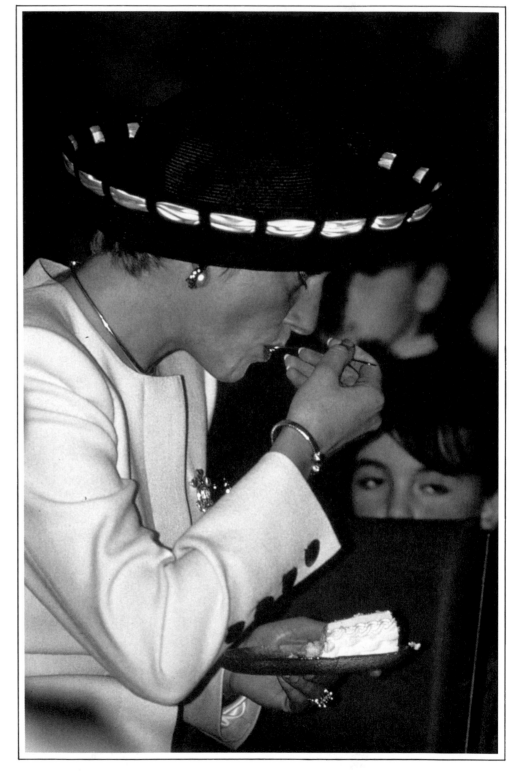

Eating in public is a cross the Princess has to bear. She actually prefers to have a substantial breakfast and then a light meal privately before appearing to eat publicly. If she actually consumed all that was put in front of her at public functions, she certainly couldn't maintain her enviable figure. Being royal is not all a piece of cake!

water and occasionally takes a course of energizing royal-jelly capsules.

She burns off the calories with the demanding fitness routine that she puts herself through and her hectic schedule of public engagements and overseas tours.

Occasional indulgences

This healthy lifestyle, combining a wholesome diet with plenty of exercise, means that neither Charles nor Diana has to diet these days. They are even able to indulge themselves occasionally with special treats. Diana adores bacon sandwiches made from Marks & Spencer's sliced white bread, as well as fish-and-chips and pizza.

The Princess is often reported to be living on a semi-vegetarian diet. But while she loves fish better than meat, she by no means eliminates meat from her diet, especially if she is eating with her small sons. She realizes how important it is for growing children to eat a healthy, balanced menu.

She will, however, sometimes send out for McDonald's hamburgers for William and Harry and treat herself to one too. She has also taken the boys to the Chicago Rib Shack which is conveniently situated near Harrods. And she is still partial to salt-and-vinegar crisps (potato chips), toffees and wine gums.

Favourite restaurants

Eating out at her favourite London restaurants, such as Le Caprice, San Lorenzo, Launceston Place and Green's champagne bar, the Princess will usually choose fish as a main course, preceded by a light starter like avocado pear. For dessert she often succumbs to a creamy sweet or sorbet.

When she is eating out privately like this, Diana is always seen to be really enjoying her food, rather than picking at it as she often does

DIANA'S LIFESTYLE-DIET

- Eat fish or white meat like chicken wherever possible instead of red meat like beef or pork.
- Eat plenty of fresh fruit and vegetables.
- Eat vegetable soup as a first course in preference to a heavier dish.
- Sometimes eat a small quantity of pasta, lightly sauced, as a main course.
- Have fruit instead of dessert at the end of a meal.
- Start the day with a breakfast of wholewheat toast or cereal.
- Substitute dry white wine or champagne for spirits or, better still, stick to mineral water or fruit juice.
- Drink at least two litres (quarts) of mineral water daily.

at public functions. She particularly enjoys San Lorenzo's raw vegetables served with a special anchovy-and-walnut sauce, followed by spaghetti with clam sauce. She also has a penchant for Chinese food and sometimes eats at the Golden Chopsticks opposite South Kensington tube station.

Hard work and will-power

Through sheer hard work and will-power, Diana has developed the ideal routine for maintaining her enviable figure and still enjoying the pasta, bread and potatoes that she loves. Her secret is moderation combined with a rigorous fitness routine to burn off the calories.

The Princess of Wales now weighs a respectable 60 kg (133 pounds, or 9½ stones), which is an ideal weight for her 1.79 m (5 foot 10½ inch), small-boned frame. She is neither too fat nor too thin. In 1989 she was voted in a survey by *Slimming* magazine the most stunning woman in the public eye, and an inspiration for all dieters.

7
Action
Woman

*W*hether she is skiing in the Swiss Alps or swimming in the pool at Buckingham Palace, the Princess of Wales is constantly on the go. She has found that the more hectic her official schedule, the more she depends upon exercise to stay relaxed and fit. Consequently, she has deliberately built it into her daily routine.

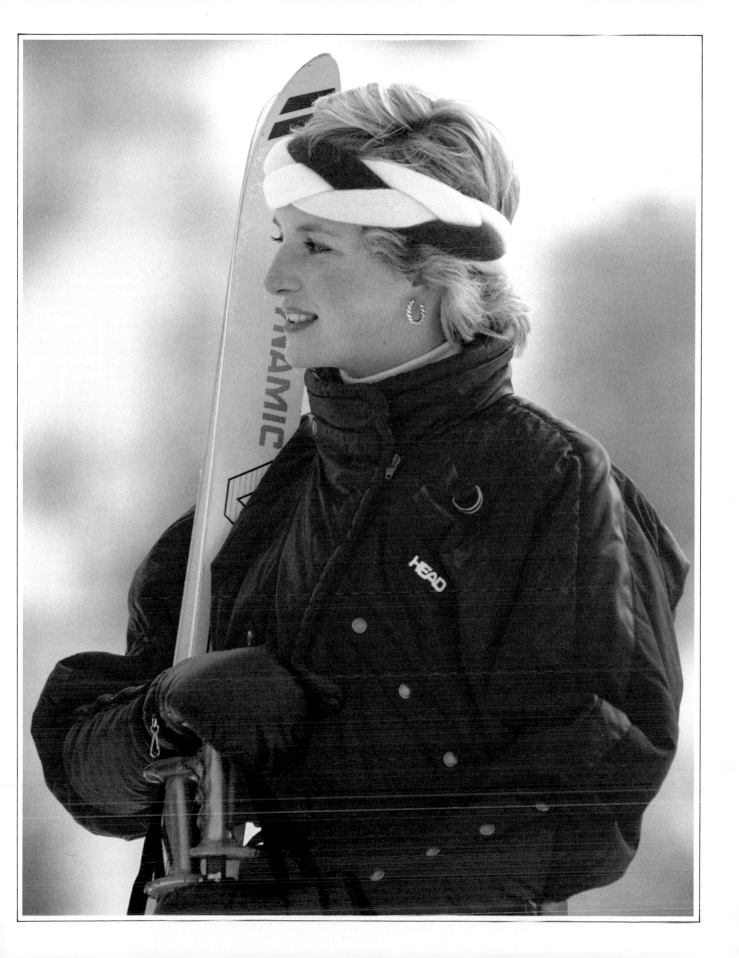

Almost all the royal family have a favourite form of exercise. It's the way that they escape from the rigours of public life and relax into a world of their own.

The Queen and Princess Anne love riding; the Queen Mother walks and, until recently, fished; the Duke of Edinburgh enjoys driving horse-drawn carriages; Princess Margaret swims at Buckingham Palace; while Prince Charles pursues a variety of sports, including hunting and polo. The Princess has taken her sports with her into the House of Windsor, not only as a form of escape and relaxation but to help her keep fit and slim.

The Princess comes from a country family, where sport is very much part of growing up. As a child Diana was very sporty. She may not have excelled particularly at school but she was an excellent swimmer and was also a keen tennis player.

A keen swimmer

At Park House in Norfolk where she spent her childhood, just across the park from Sandringham, there was a heated swimming pool which the younger princes used too when they were staying at Sandringham. The young Lady Diana was renowned for her smooth swallow-diving.

Today, Diana still loves to swim, as much for relaxation as for fitness. When she's at Kensington Palace, she's up and out by 7.00 am to drive over to Buckingham Palace, wearing her tracksuit over her swimsuit. There she fits in a quick twenty to thirty lengths, alternating between backstroke and breast-stroke.

At Highgrove, where Charles and Diana spend their weekends, there is a heated outdoor pool. When she is at Sandringham with the rest of the royal family on summer and Christmas holidays, Diana misses her swim so much that she now takes her children to a local club, the Knights Hill Health and Leisure Club in Kings Lynn, which has an indoor pool. There she puts herself through a stringent swim and workout routine to counteract the effects of over-indulging *en famille* during the holidays. And when they are at Balmoral, Diana pops along to the Craigendarroch Hotel and Country Club in nearby Ballater for a similar swim and workout with her children.

When she's on tour abroad, Diana always tries to fit in an early-morning dip. She especially enjoys her holidays in Majorca with the Spanish royal family; on Richard Branson's private Caribbean island of Necker; and on the royal yacht *Britannia*, where she can swim and sunbathe too.

The perfect exercise

Swimming is one of the very best exercises and is frequently recommended by doctors for patients with a tendency to high blood pressure and heart complaints. Not only does it stretch and tone the whole body, but it soothes the mind; it is an excellent antidote to stress.

The rhythmic movements of swimming place a demand on the heart and lungs, which helps build endurance, and also on virtually all the body's major muscle groups. It puts less stress on the body's tendons, ligaments and joints than running or other endurance activities do.

Diana has in the past suffered from a bad back, but swimming is one of the few exercises that does not place a burden on the spine, hips, knees and other joints. This is because the natural buoyancy of the body in water relieves it of weight-bearing stresses.

Tennis-mad

Diana also excelled at tennis at school, although not quite to the standard of her mother, who actually got through to the Wimbledon semi-finals before her marriage. Diana would watch Wimbledon avidly on television at school and was taken there annually for the first Saturday of each season by her mother. Now she is able to watch the Wimbledon semi-finals and the finals from the comfort of the Royal Box.

The Princess might well have joined the rather sedate Hurlingham Club in west London or the swanky Roehampton in Putney to play tennis. Instead, she belongs to the Vanderbilt Club, which is situated in an altogether unprepossessing part of London. With no sign outside to identify it, it is in a tiny street of red-brick houses just off London's Shepherd's Bush Green, rather than in elegant parklands.

But walk up four slippery flights of stairs and you're in another world. The hub of the club is a cosy reception-cum-lounge area furnished with comfortable sofas covered with pastel prints; a well-stocked corner bar dispenses filter coffee in china cups embellished with crossed rackets, as well as food and alcohol. Classical music plays in the background.

The adjacent boutique sells the most coveted sports item in London – a simple red or emerald green sweatshirt embroidered with the magic word Vanderbilt.

A very private club

The view through tinted glass is of the number one court – the court for show-offs – with its carpet-like surface of green turf that is so comfortable you can actually play on it in your bare feet (although it's not recommended). All the other seven courts are totally secluded: each has private access so that it is perfectly possible to play in complete secrecy. The giveaway is that central lounge area where paths cross and people linger to socialize. The atmosphere of the Vanderbilt is at once relaxed, friendly and sociable – not at all the sweaty, spartan atmosphere of the usual tennis club.

SWIM AND SLIM

As Princess Diana has discovered, swimming is the perfect all-round exercise. Here are some tips to help you benefit from it as much as possible.

1 Each stroke uses different muscles, and some burn off calories faster than others. From most vigorous to least vigorous, the strokes are: butterfly, front crawl, back crawl, breast-stroke and side-stroke.

2 Begin your swimming programme by swimming 100 metres (109 yards) – four lengths of a 25-metre (27-yard) pool with a one-minute rest period between each length. As you gain confidence and swimming ability, gradually increase the number of lengths you can do continuously. By the second or third week you may be able to swim 50 metres (54 yards) with a one-minute rest, followed by two 25-metre (27-yard) swims with a one-minute rest after each, followed by one more 50-metre (54-yard) swim.

3 To build endurance, shorten the rest period and increase the length of your continuous swim.

4 A more rigorous variation is "pyramids" – a series of lengths in ascending and then descending numbers. You can swim 1,600 metres (1,750 yards) for example, in a "pyramid eight": one length followed by a rest period then two lengths, and so on up to eight, then back down. At the height of the pyramid you should feel close to fatigue, but as the numbers decrease you will feel stronger and can even increase your swimming intensity.

5 You can build both endurance and speed with interval training, which consists of a timed swim alternating with a timed rest. For instance, if you can swim 50 metres (54 yards) in less than one minute, give yourself intervals of one minute, 15 seconds. Swim the distance as fast as you can, then rest for the remaining time: if you swim it in 50 seconds you have 25 seconds to rest

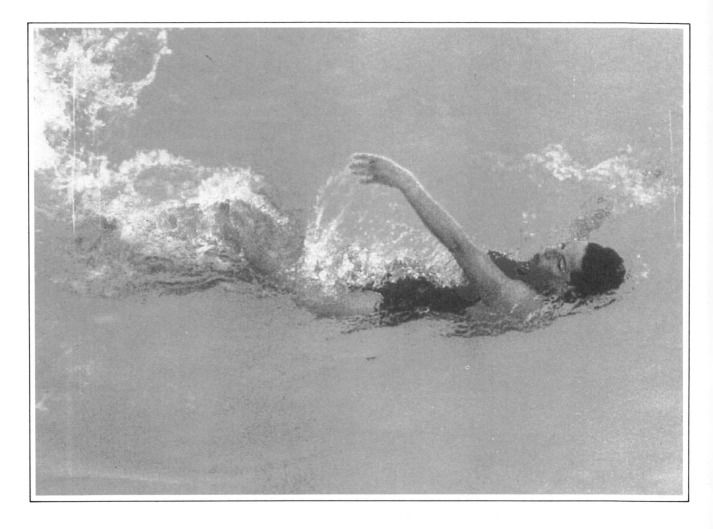

Diana tries to fit in a swim wherever she is. Her country home has an outdoor pool, and in London
she uses the indoor pool at Buckingham Palace.

It's not surprising that the club is unique. It is owned and run by Old Etonian and ex-Harrow schoolmaster Charles Swallow, a rackets expert and Oxford University Triple Blue (rackets, tennis, squash). Charming and debonair, he is ably assisted by his wife, hence the friendly family atmosphere.

The Vanderbilt Club is housed in vast buildings built in 1908 for the Great White City Franco-British Exhibition. The walls have been hung with tarpaulins for privacy, yet the glass roofs allow daylight play all-year-round.

Charles Swallow initially coached the Princess personally and has become a close friend, lunching with her at Kensington Palace. She gave him a hand-knitted sweater with a tennis racket motif for his fiftieth birthday.

The Princess was introduced to the "Vandy" by the Marquis of Douro's wife Antonia; she joined by paying a signing-on fee of £650 ($1,170) and a £500 ($900) annual subscription. Now, with Prince Harry and Prince

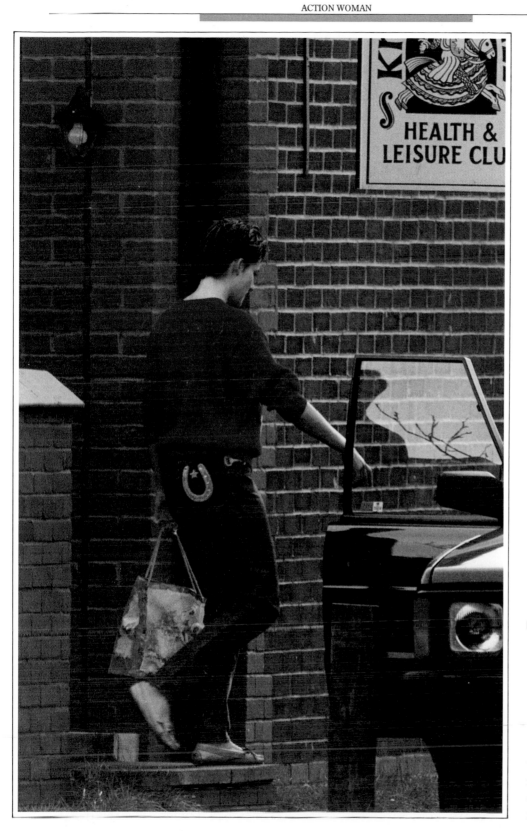

Swimming is one of the Princess's favourite ways of unwinding and keeping trim. Even when she's holidaying in Norfolk on the remote Sandringham estate with the rest of the royal family, Diana manages to escape for a swim at a nearby leisure club.

William playing there too, she opts for the full family membership of £1,450 ($2,610) with an annual subscription of £1,195 ($2,151).

"With just over 1,000 members, people are treated here as people rather than bodies," says Charles Swallow, "and people are desperate to be able to play tennis indoors in London."

Elite membership

The club's elite members (Gayle Hunnicut and her husband Simon Jenkins, editor of *The Times;* Winston Churchill MP; and Virginia Wade are just a few of the club's patrons) enjoy all the ancillary services provided. As well as fifteen of the country's best tennis professionals as coaches, there are a fully equipped gym, a snooker table and a fulltime physiotherapist. There is also a jolly social programme of matches followed by dinners at the club.

Diana has been coached not only by Charles Swallow, but also, more recently, by ex-international ice-hockey star Rex Seymour-Lynn, who teaches the young princes too, and her game has improved enormously. She plays there every ten days or so, schedule-permitting, and has also taken aerobic classes from the club's exercise guru Jan Robinson, who retired at the end of 1991.

"She hadn't played a great deal when she was younger, and she does it primarily for the exercise," says Charles Swallow. "She's now become a respectable player and well able to play here in the rallies. But as she only comes once every ten days or so, it's difficult for her to work on a particular shot."

Prince Harry and Prince William are now learning to play too, and the Princess has even asked German star Steffi Graf if she can coach William a little.

"She has asked me several times if I can give her son an hour's lesson," Steffi has said. "She has told me that he is absolutely mad about tennis. Of course I shall treat him more gently than I did Martina Navratilova."

Winning combination

In 1988, Steffi Graf played a much publicized mixed-doubles match at the Vanderbilt with Diana, who said before they began, "I'm very nervous. I'm not very good, you know. But I love the game." They beat two of the the club's male players 6-5. And afterwards Steffi said how surprised she was at the Princess's game.

TENNIS TIPS FROM DIANA'S COACH

Charles Swallow, owner of the Vanderbilt Club, where Princess Diana plays tennis, helped her to improve her game dramatically. Here are some of his tips.

- If you feel inspired to take to the tennis courts for the first time since your schooldays, remember that the game has changed drastically. Rackets made using modern technology are much more dangerous weapons and give powerful vibrations that can transmit into your arms with a far greater degree of injuries, such as tennis elbow.
- Anyone over thirty should always warm up before actually playing. Don't go into it cold.
- Hit the ball very softly at first and then gradually work up into hard shots. It's mad to start playing hard from the start. Tennis should be played at least two to three times a week to tone your muscles and aid weight loss.
- A tennis ball is much more difficult to hit than a squash ball. Take each learning step one at a time. The jump from being coached into playing games is the biggest leap.
- The two essential qualities for a tennis player are an eye for the ball and an ability to move quickly on the feet. I can tell if a child of three or four has the ability to be a tennis player by its ability to move on its feet.

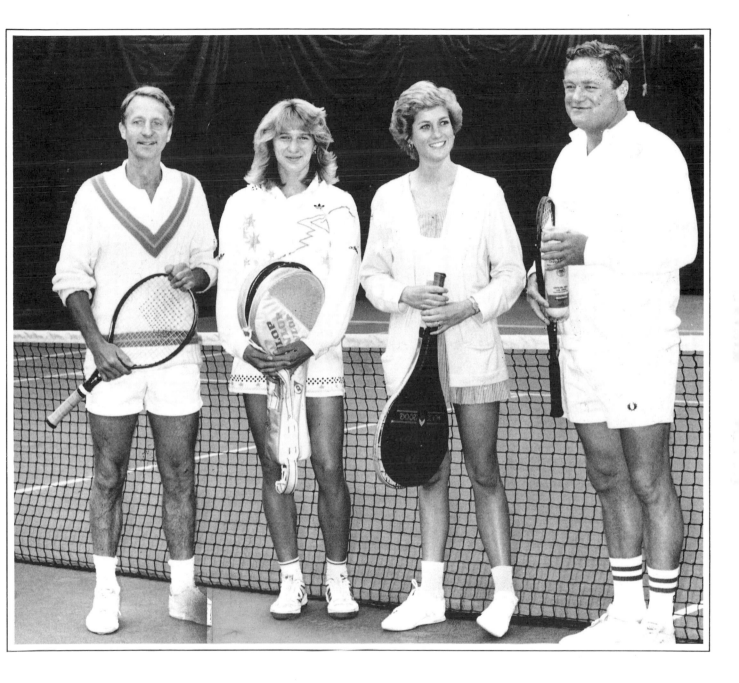

The Princess of Wales is an ace tennis player of sufficient standard to take on champion Steffi Graf in a game of mixed doubles in 1988. They are seen afterwards at London's Vanderbilt Club, where Diana plays regularly. The owner of the club, Charles Swallow (far right), has personally coached Diana, and her playing has improved enormously.

"She has a good serve and forehand, but perhaps her backhand needs a little work."

Diana is an honorary member of the All-England Lawn Tennis and Croquet Club, Britain's most important tennis club which was founded in 1877 and which is responsible for holding Wimbledon. She is also an honorary member of the David Lloyd Slazenger Club at Hounslow in Middlesex.

The Princess does not appear to like playing on her own court at Highgrove but has been known to play on the court at the Hare and Hounds Hotel at nearby Westonbirt.

A passion for dance

Diana's other great passion is dance. As a child she dreamed of becoming a ballerina and she still admits to being "obsessed" with it. She started dancing lessons when she was just three-and-a-half years old. On school expeditions she went to see *Sleeping Beauty, Giselle* and *Coppelia,* waiting for hours with other fans at the stage door to get autographs from the dancers. *Swan Lake* she saw over and over again.

Unfortunately, Diana's ambition to become a professional dancer was quickly nipped in the bud when she became too tall. "I overshot the height by a long way," she has said. "I couldn't imagine some man trying to lift me up above his arms."

In her bachelor-girl days, Diana continued to dance, taking tap dancing, jazz dance and keep-fit classes at the Dance Centre in Covent Garden and adult classes at the Vacani Dance School where she worked.

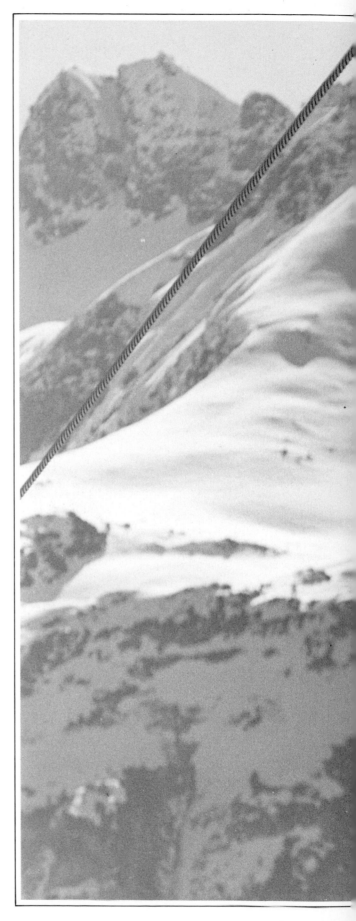

Family skiing holidays are another form of escape from a hectic regime of official engagements. Skiing is a favourite sport of both Princess Diana and Prince Charles, as well as their two boys.

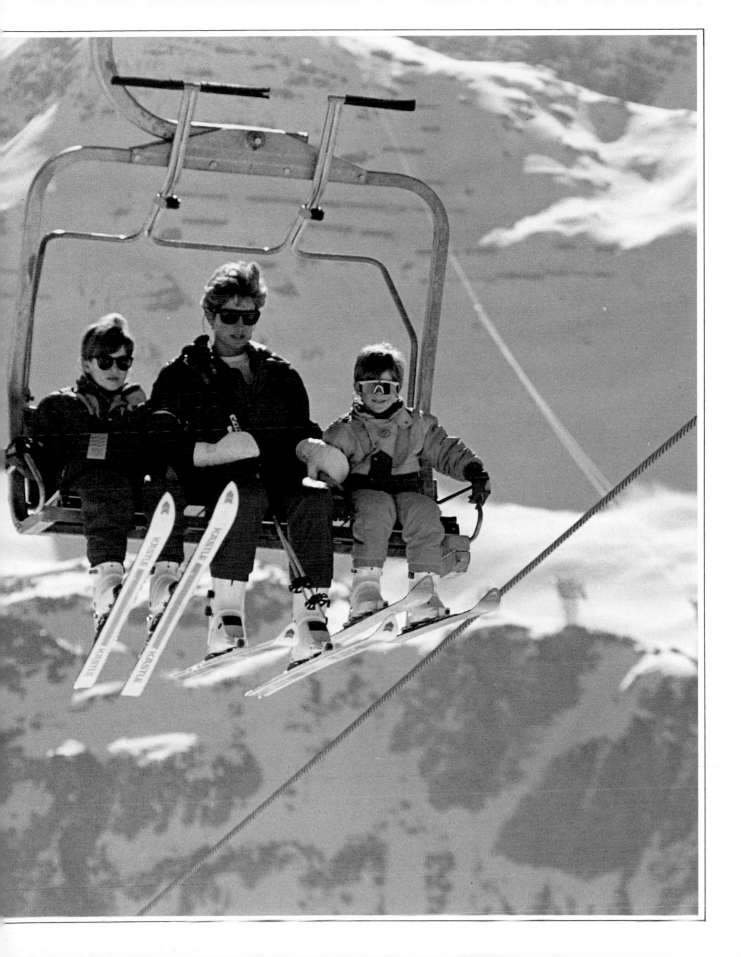

After her engagement, when she was living at Buckingham Palace, she took hour-long ballet lessons twice a week in the Throne Room. Her instructor was the elderly Miss Snipp, who had been her dance teacher at West Heath School in Kent and who had given her piano lessons.

Diana would even round off each session by tap dancing, just as she used to do as a child on the chequered black-and-white marble floor of the grand entrance hall to Wootton Hall, her family home.

Over the years, the Princess has continued with her dancing as much as time will allow. It is obviously very difficult for her to attend regular lessons as she used to do, since these can frequently be interrupted by a royal tour. Instead she now does dance-exercise at least twice a week under the personal tuition of her trainer Carolan Brown (see page 98).

In 1983, the Princess took six weeks of lessons at the studio of Dame Merle Park, Principal of the Royal Ballet and Director of the Royal Ballet School. And in 1988, in order to surprise Prince Charles with a present of a video of herself dancing, she had instruction from award-winning choreographer Gillian Lynne.

For two years Diana took regular private lessons from Anne Allan, former ballet mistress with the London City Ballet, behind drawn blinds at the dance studios of the English National Ballet near the Royal Albert Hall. Unfortunately, these had to stop when Anne moved back to her native Scotland.

Taking to the stage

The nearest the Princess has got to dancing professionally was when she took to the stage of the Royal Opera House at Covent Garden with the petite cockney dancer Wayne Sleep, to the astonishment of the audience, and especially Prince Charles.

Wayne had secretly coached Diana in their high-kicking, soft-shoe-tapping routine both at Kensington Palace and over the telephone. They took eight curtain calls, and Wayne said later, "Diana is a true performer. When she was dancing with me that one time, she was electric." Wayne and the Princess have remained friends ever since.

To many people, Wayne Sleep epitomizes the popular interest in dance as an exercise that began in the Eighties. As he says himself, "Dance has been my life since I was twelve years old, so it has been really exciting for me to witness the current dance boom, with thousands of people of all ages getting the same sort of pleasure from it as I do, taking classes in tap or jazz or contemporary for their own sake, as well as for keeping fit.

"There's no doubt that dance is a great way of keeping fit. It keeps you young, it gets your body working at its best with your muscles in tune, and it's a great feeling, knowing that your body can do anything you want it to do."

The Princess may not have time to take professional dance lessons these days, but she

SUPER SPORT

Sports provide a fun way to take exercise. Because they are done primarily for enjoyment, their benefits to the body seem like a bonus. Yet they are usually of considerable value. Tennis, for example, which is regularly played by Diana, tones up the muscles of the calves, thighs and buttocks; strengthens the muscles of the arms, shoulders, chest, waist and back; and improves upper-body flexibility. Even horse riding, which she occasionally does, works the muscles of the inner thighs and calves and the hips, stomach, waist and back.

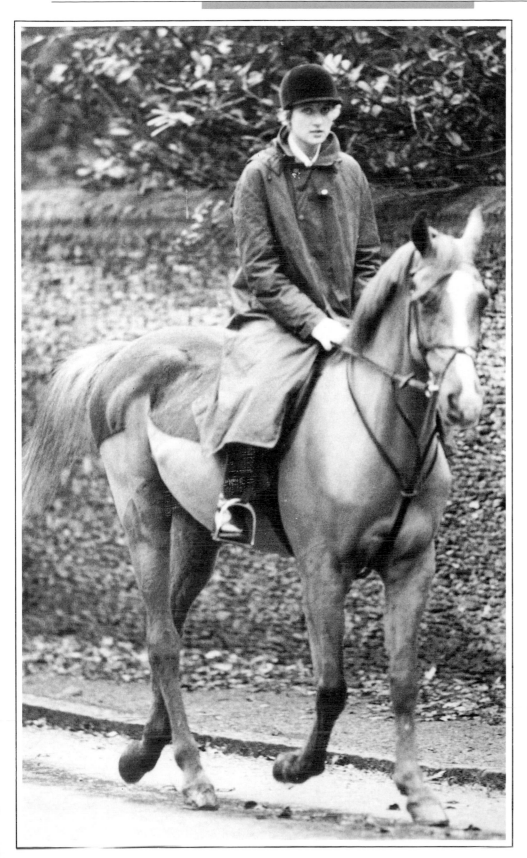

Princess Diana has not really enjoyed horse riding since she fell off her pony as a small child. However, she does get in the saddle occasionally. Here she is pictured riding on a rainy day at Sandringham.

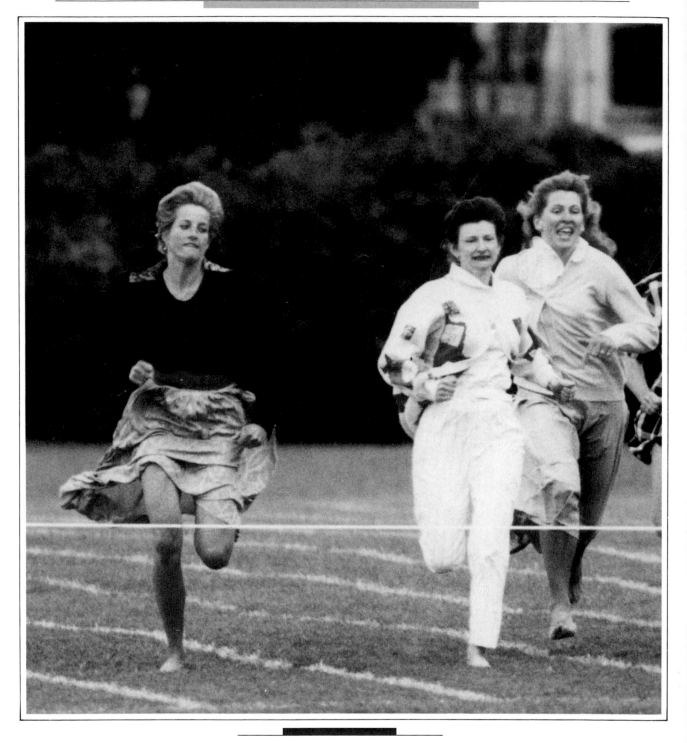

Princess Diana never fails to take part in her sons' end-of-term parents' day race and is very
often the first past the winning post. It's a sign of her all-round aptitude for all aspects of sport,
either solo or competitive.

loves to take to the dance floor at every possible opportunity.

Her greatest thrill was a spell of disco-dancing to "Saturday Night Fever" with John Travolta at a White House banquet which was given by the Reagans.

Ivan Nagy, the Hungarian-born Artistic Director of the English National Ballet who has danced with prima ballerinas Natalia Makarova and Margot Fonteyn, was quoted after dancing with the Princess as saying, "She's wonderful. She is the most light-footed dancer I have ever partnered."

The Princess, who is patron of both the English National Ballet and the London City Ballet, loves nothing better than to go round to their studios to talk to the dancers, taking a great interest in their problems and injuries. She has travelled with the London City Ballet to both Oslo and Washington in order to help raise desperately needed funds for the company, which does not receive funding from the Arts Council.

Other sporting interests

Unlike most of the royal family, Diana is not a horsy person. She lost her nerve for riding when, at the age of eight, she fell off her pony and broke her arm. Occasionally, Diana has been seen back in the saddle, riding with the Queen. She even, unsuccessfully, tried hunting, to please her husband.

Until the dramatic death of Major Hugh Lindsay on their 1988 skiing holiday in a party which included the Duke and Duchess of York, the Princess, like her husband, was an avid skier. She was also a very competent one, but the tragic incident seems to have soured the sport for her, and she has spent much less time on the slopes since. However, it looks as though the enthusiasm of Prince William and Prince Harry may rekindle her interest in skiing.

VALUE OF THE ROYAL EXERCISE

With her demanding lifestyle, the Princess of Wales relies on exercise to keep looking and feeling good. Taking regular, vigorous exercise – preferably at least three thirty minute sessions a week – has innumerable benefits and will help you just as it has the future Queen of England. Benefits of exercise in general include: helping keep your weight down; toning the body; making you stronger and more supple; improving skin, nails and hair; increasing energy levels; boosting the immune system, which makes you healthier; strengthening the heart and lungs; sharpening the brain; aiding relaxation; alleviating stress and fatigue.

SWIMMING Good for conditioning the whole body, particularly the upper torso, when done strenuously. Extremely low injury rate and can be done by people with orthopedic injuries or disabilities. A solitary exercise, it can lead sometimes to ear infections.

CALORIES BURNED PER HALF-HOUR ACTIVITY
25 metres (27 yards) per minute: 165 Calories
40 metres (44 yards) per minute: 240 Calories
50 metres (54 yards) per minute: 345 Calories

AEROBICS Good exercise that can be done either in a class or alone. Can be used to work out all parts of the body. Relatively high injury rate in lower leg and foot for high-impact aerobics, but with lower-impact aerobics it is harder to raise heart beat. Useful weight-bearing exercise in order to help prevent osteoporosis occurring later in life.

CALORIES BURNED PER HALF-HOUR ACTIVITY
light: 120 Calories: moderate: 200 Calories; vigorous: 300 Calories

SKIING Good exercise for toning the total body but there's a relatively high injury rate and the equipment is expensive. Travel involved in getting to snowy climes is another factor.

CALORIES BURNED PER HALF-HOUR ACTIVITY
Light: 200 Calories; moderate: 300 Calories; vigorous: 410 Calories or more.

8

Re-shaping the Royal Curves

D *ieting alone was not enough to effect the transformation from an awkward, plump teenager into one of the world's great beauties. In order to make her fairy-tale metamorphosis complete, the Princess of Wales has worked hard, with the help of specific exercise routines and a personal trainer, to dramatically remodel her figure.*

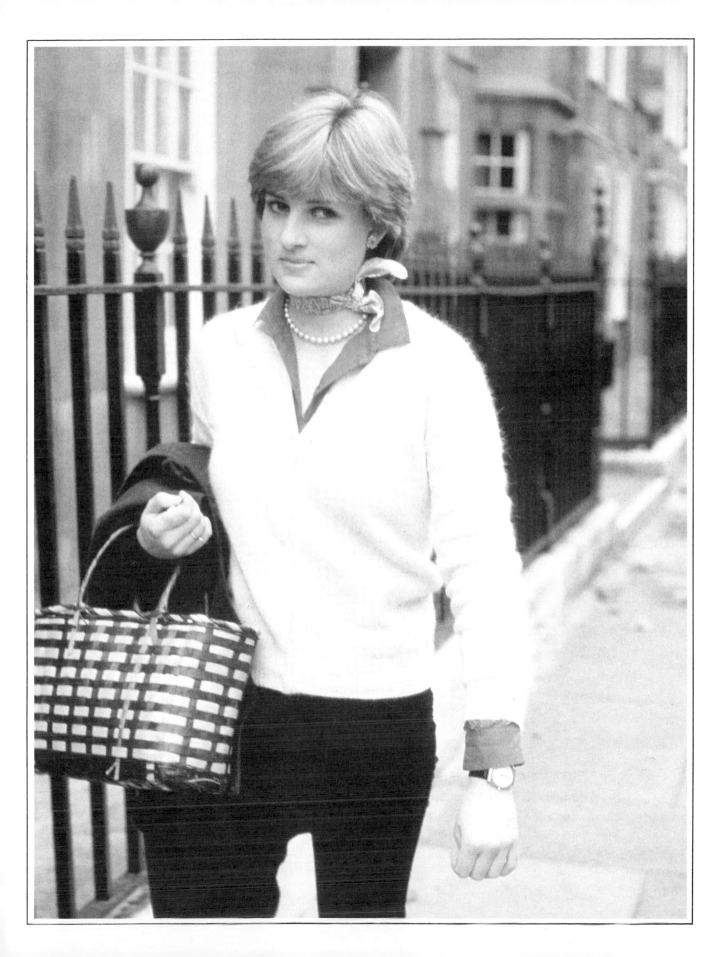

These days, it is perfectly possible to have the body of your dreams. The Princess of Wales has proved this without a doubt. In just a few years, she has transformed herself from a gawky girl into a ravishing beauty.

Today she is svelte and slim without being too skinny. Toned and trimmed with perfect posture, the Princess of Wales is the most photographed woman in the world. Instead of stooping to disguise her height, as she used to do, Diana stands proud and tall to show off her couture clothes.

The power of determination

But even with the world's experts in diet and exercise at her disposal, the Princess of Wales has proved that there is no easy solution to figure problems. Time and money help, of course, but at the end of the day it amounts to two things – determination to be what you want to be, and hard work.

With all of the Princess's efforts to present her body in the best possible way, she has proved that it is more a matter of technique and regular routine than having a personal trainer, although the Princess does enjoy this currently fashionable indulgence. It is the simple but regular forms of body reshaping which she has fitted into her everyday schedule that have effected the major transformations.

Even the sports-mad Princess of Wales needs special additional daily exercises to keep her figure in perfect shape. Despite her demanding routine of swimming, tennis and dance-exercise, she still needs extra help. And like most exercise-addicted people, she desperately needs an easy alternative to sport when she's unable through travelling to participate with the usual regularity.

After her early morning swim, the Princess returns home for an intensive workout, either with her personal trainer Carolan Brown or using one of Carolan's three videos. Her addiction to training is such that it's not restricted to the early morning – if she is unable to see Carolan then, she will make sure she sees her for their workout at some time during the day, at least two or three times a week.

Stepping out

Diana first met Carolan in 1990. Using the pseudonym Sally Hastings, Diana checked herself into the LA Fitness club in Old Isleworth, Middlesex, a quiet west London suburban backwater. She had read in a magazine of its new American exercise system using step-boxes which was being pioneered in Britain by studio director Carolan Brown. Diana worked hard in the gym, and classmates were impressed at how adept the Princess was at exercise and movement.

Since then she has managed to persuade Carolan Brown to visit her personally at Kensington Palace where they follow a punishing routine of personal exercises in privacy. The exercises done on a step-box, which burn up the calories relatively fast, are equivalent to running at 11 km (7 miles) an hour.

Jogging in the park

Sometimes the Princess will nip out of Kensington Palace at around 9.00 am for a jog in Kensington Gardens, the public park surrounding the Palace, just as the pop star Madonna does when she is in London. But while both wear tracksuit or shorts, and are accompanied by bodyguards puffing behind them, Diana's jog will go largely unnoticed while Madonna's is very much a full media affair. If it's raining, Diana will have the equivalent of a 3-km (2-mile) walk on her mechanical treadmill machine instead.

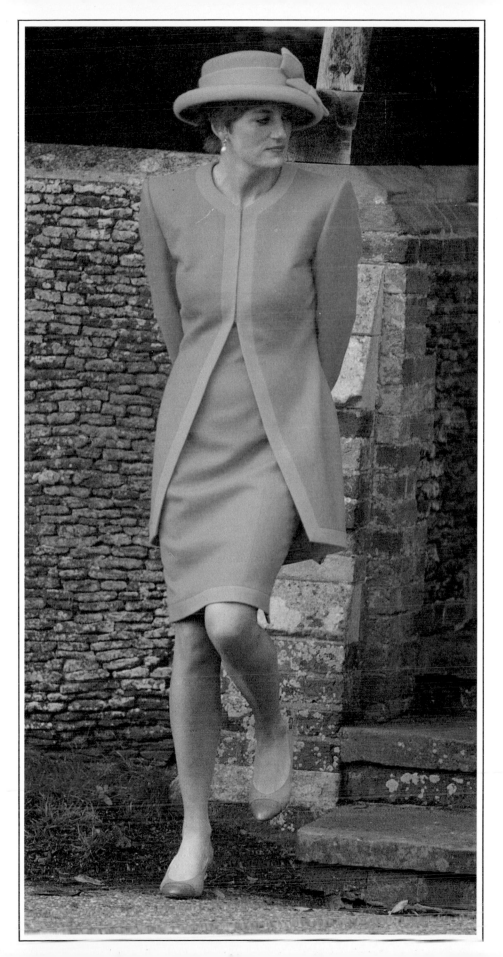

The Princess of Wales may have the figure of a model, but she works hard at keeping it that way. Every week she sees her personal trainer Carolan Brown at least three times, and together they go through a gruelling routine of dance exercise and step aerobics.

STEP AEROBICS

Here are the basics of a step-aerobic routine, devised by Princess Diana's trainer Carolan Brown, using an adjustable step-box, or "body board".

1 Stand with feet together, shoulders back and down, buttocks tucked under and knees slightly bent. Contract your stomach and buttock muscles as you step up. Hands can be on your hips or by your sides.

2 As you step up, lean into the movement with your whole body; avoid ever leaning backwards. Look straight ahead and not down. Your feet should be placed in the centre of the box – do not allow them to overhang.

4 As you step back off the box you should land gently on the ball of the foot and roll onto the heel. Never step off the box forwards, nor step onto it backwards. Now try stepping up eight times leading with the right foot. On the eighth step,

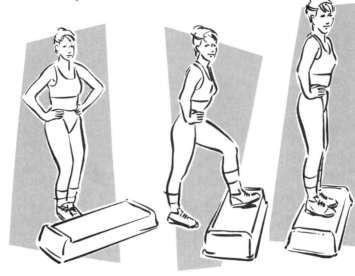

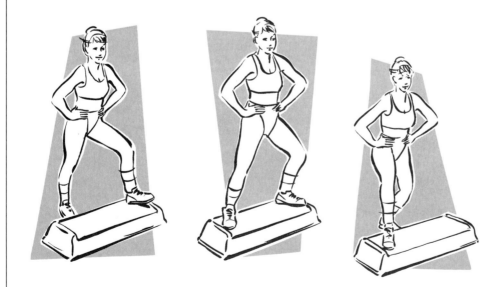

tap the left foot and repeat eight times leading with the left. (Avoid favouring one leg over the other – the tap is the key to changing legs.)

5 Another step is the wide step. Leaning into the movement, step onto the lefthand edge of the box.

6 Now bring the right foot up onto the righthand edge of the box.

7 Step off the box with the left foot, remembering to land on the ball of the foot first. Try this eight times leading with the left foot. On the eighth step, tap the right foot, then repeat eight times leading with the right. Your feet should return to the centre after each step.

A FLATTER STOMACH

These stomach-toning exercises were devised by Princess Diana's personal trainer, Carolan Brown. When doing them, be sure to breathe out when you are exerting, and breathe in when you're relaxing. Keep your back flat against the floor rather than arching it, and concentrate on using your abdominal muscles to do the work, rather than your back or neck.

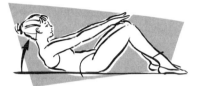

1 Lie on your back with your knees bent, your feet the width of your hips apart and your arms by your side. Slowly lift your shoulders off the floor, and stretch your hands towards the tops of your knees. To keep your head in the right position, pretend you have an apple under your chin. Slowly lower back to the floor.

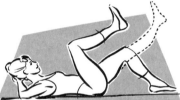

2 Lie on your back with one foot on the floor and the knee bent, and the other leg lifted with the knee bent. Start with your head lifted about 2 cm (1 inch) from the floor, then raise your shoulders and simultaneously extend the raised leg, keeping thighs parallel. Slowly bend your leg back and lower your shoulders down to the starting position (ie just above the floor). Do this eight times for one leg, before repeating for the other leg.

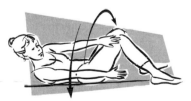

3 Lie on your back with your knees bent, your feet the width of your shoulders apart, your arms and hands extended, and your head and shoulders raised. Raise the upper body and twist it, taking your arms to the right so that the left hand touches the outside of the right knee. Return to starting position and repeat to other side.

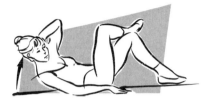

4 Lie on your back with your left knee bent and left foot on the floor, your right foot resting on your left knee, and your left hand behind your head, elbow pointing outwards (not forward). Now raise your left shoulder towards your right knee (leading with the shoulder, not the elbow). Slowly lower to starting position. Do eight times, then repeat for the other side.

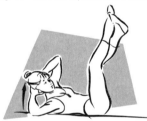

5 Lie on your back with your legs at right angles to the floor, knees bent slightly and ankles crossed. Your hands should be behind your head. Raise your left shoulder towards your right knee (leading with the shoulder, not the elbow). Slowly lower to starting position. Do eight times then repeat for the other side.

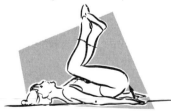

6 Lie on your back with your legs raised, knees bent and ankles crossed. Arms should be on the floor. Use your abdominal muscles, not leg muscles, to slowly bring your knees towards your chest then take them back to the starting position.

9

Royal Fringe Benefits

That radiant royal glow is based on sheer good health. Almost the entire royal family were hooked on homeopathy and other alternative medicines long before they became fashionable. Zone therapy is a favourite, and other offbeat cures favoured by the Princess of Wales include colonic irrigation, acupuncture, t'ai chi and shiatsu massage.

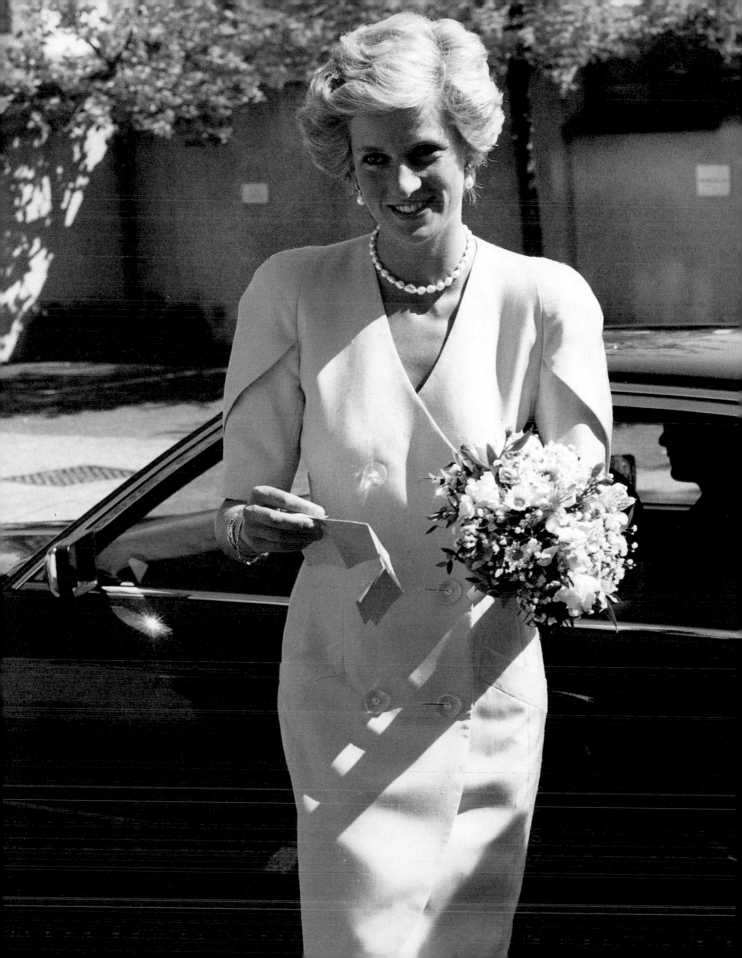

Both the Queen and Prince Charles had a deep and well-informed knowledge of alternative medicine long before it became as fashionable as it has today. They are well ahead of the field in terms of their understanding and use of homeopathy and other alternative forms of medicine.

Charles told the Royal College of General Practitioners in 1990 that he was saddened by the mistrustful attitudes of doctors to complementary medicine. "What I am in favour of," he said, "is the harnessing of the best aspects of ancient and modern medicine to contribute towards the most effective healing of the patient's mind and body."

Homeopathy

The royal devotion to homeopathy underlines their whole attitude to self-improvement the natural way. Ten years ago homeopathic medicine was regarded as an almost crankish obsession. Today, homeopathic cures can be bought over the counter at most high-street chemists (drugstores) and also have a fierce following among the rich and famous.

To the Princess, these simple natural remedies provide the basis for the inner health that is at the heart of her glowing beauty.

While Nelson's Pharmacy held the royal warrants until a few years ago (and still supply the royal family), once they had become involved in large-scale manufacturing the warrants were transferred to the much smaller Ainsworth Pharmacy. Situated in New Cavendish Street in London's West End, they now hold the warrants of the Queen, the Queen Mother and Prince Charles.

Ainsworth's manager Mr Pinkus says that while homeopathic medicine has long been fashionable with the crowned heads of Europe, it has only now enjoyed a revival. A highly personalized form of medicine (Ainsworth's alone produce 3,000 to 4,000 individual remedies), it is prescribed to the royal family by their own physician Dr Ronald Davey.

Homeopathy is the age-old medical practice of treating like with like – in other words, treating an illness with a substance that produces similar symptoms to those displayed by the person who is ill. Unlike current medicine, which sees symptoms as a direct manifestation of the illness, homeopathy sees the symptoms as the body's reaction against the illness as it attempts to heal itself. Therefore, treatment with a substance that would cause the same symptoms if given in larger doses is believed to actually strengthen the body's defences, so it can heal itself more easily.

Homeopathy is essentially a natural healing process concentrating on treating the patient, rather than the illness. All homeopathic remedies are based on plants or other natural substances. Many would be poisonous if taken in large doses, but they are diluted so much – often down to less than one part in a million – that they become harmless. Yet, astonishingly, they retain their effectiveness.

Homeopathists believe that an illness is not the same from person to person, since everybody responds to it in a different way. Homeopathic medicines are prescribed individually after the doctor has studied the whole person, including their basic temperament and responses.

Although there are more than 2,000 homeopathic remedies, only a small number are commonly employed. For instance, arsenic can help to cure burning pains in the stomach, belladonna may be used for treating air sickness, and sulphur can help psoriasis.

Colonic irrigation

The Princess of Wales has resorted to one of the most fashionable – and controversial – of alternative medical practices, colonic irrigation, which involves washing out the bowels. She visits the Hale Clinic in London's Regent's Park, which was opened by the Prince of Wales in 1988.

Popular in the Twenties, colonic irrigation is enjoying a revival in the New Age Nineties. Enthusiasts range from Hollywood film stars to London society.

Its advocates claim that the bowels are a source of pollution of the "inner environment", making a person feel lethargic and bloated. Washing out the waste matter is said to leave a person feeling brighter and lighter. Many chic New Yorkers use it as an instant slimming cure before an important social event, saying that it not only flattens their stomachs but noticeably improves their complexions.

However, bowel specialists are sceptical of the efficacy and even the safety of the practice. They consider it to be both unnecessary and ineffective for people who are healthy and unconstipated, since the digestive system is very efficiently designed to cleanse itself. They stress that the colon does not release toxins into the bloodstream, contrary to colonic irrigation theory.

Furthermore, colonics can prove positively dangerous, they maintain, because of the risk of injuring the colon walls or even rupturing the colon, as well as the possibility of introducing infection, or upsetting the body fluid balance. They claim that it should only be used in hospitals as a form of treatment for chronic constipation or colostomies.

The treatment involves lying on a couch beneath a tank of water. A large stainless steel machine with a number of plastic tubes leading from it pumps water into the body via the rectum and then sucks out the waste matter down another tube. About 45 litres (10 Imperial gallons, or 12 US gallons) of water is used in each treatment. The water is filtered and at body temperature.

Years of stored-up faecal matter, mucous deposits and other waste matter are flushed out. After the treatment, patients are given a drink containing acidophilus micro-organisms to restore the correct culture to the intestines.

A series of irrigations at weekly intervals is initially recommended. The technique, it is claimed by its advocates, will improve not only elimination but also the body's response to dietary, homeopathic, herbal, manipulative and other therapies.

In fact, there is nothing new about colonics. The Egyptians were performing a type of colonic irrigation in 1500 BC, while in Victorian times colonics were popular with people from all walks of life, from workmen to royalty.

The Colonic International Association claims that colonics can be used to help such conditions as halitosis, headaches, haemorrhoids, allergies, tiredness, depression, schizophrenia, flatulence, ME (myalgic encephalomyelitis), candida and asthma.

Zone therapy

Another area of fringe medicine patronized by royalty (including the Princess), politicians, show business celebrities and businessmen is zone therapy. Joseph Corvo, the leading practitioner of zone therapy, emphasizes that this is not an alternative medicine but is complementary to conventional medicine. It was invented by a doctor, and Corvo's patients are often recommended to him by doctors.

In his modest flat in London's Bayswater where he both lives and practises, Corvo is understandably discreet about his clientele, which includes not only the Princess of Wales, and at least two other royals, but also several leading members of the Government. However, there is no mistaking the Christmas card

ZONE THERAPY PRESSURE POINTS

Princess Diana and some other members of the royal family are among the many people who have visited Joseph Corvo for zone therapy. Massaging the appropriate pressure points on the hands, feet, face, ears, neck and tongue is the basis of zone therapy. Each zone encompasses the organs, glands and nervous systems of a particular area of the body. The zones correspond to the body's ten main electromagnetic currents, and massaging the pressure points is said to help the current flow more freely. The pressure points of the hands and feet are shown here.

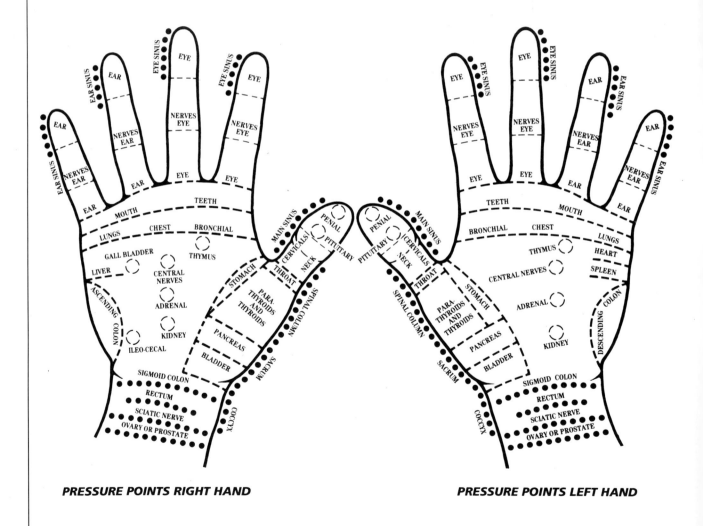

PRESSURE POINTS RIGHT HAND

PRESSURE POINTS LEFT HAND

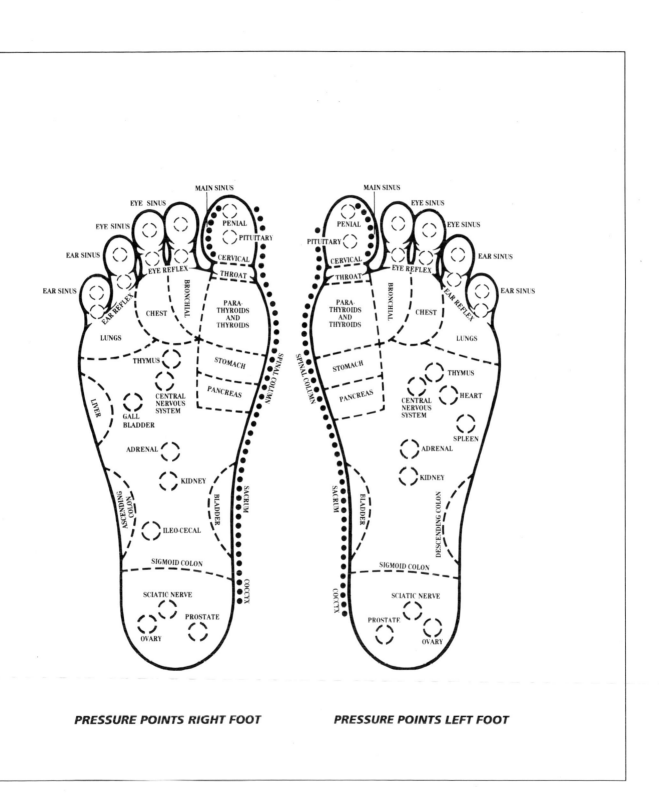

PRESSURE POINTS RIGHT FOOT   **PRESSURE POINTS LEFT FOOT**

from Prince Charles which takes pride of place on his mantelpiece.

The Princess of Wales was introduced to Joseph Corvo by her step-grandmother, the author Barbara Cartland, who swears by his magic touch. "Joseph Corvo is unique and a phenomenon," says Barbara Cartland. "When I first met Joseph, having been told about him by the Duke of Abercorn, I realized at once he was different to anyone I had ever met. What he does is to make one physically well, and also to lift one specifically."

Zone therapy was developed in America in the Sixties and Joseph Corvo, who has been practising it for thirty years, is now the world's most famous practitioner. In the most simplistic terms, it is the art of stimulating the organs through pressure-point massage. But, says Corvo, it is very different from the ancient Oriental art of reflexology.

Treatments involve applying pressure over the appropriate nerve endings in the body to release harmful toxins – the crystalline deposits which build up at nerve endings due to the normal stresses and strains of everyday life and which impair the free flow of the body's electromagnetic currents. The area of the body that each of these ten currents covers is called a zone. Running side by side from head to toe, the zones encompass all the organs, glands and nervous systems. When the flow of any of the electromagnetic currents is blocked, health and appearance suffer in the corresponding parts of the body.

Corvo claims that his treatments can make patients look and feel as much as twenty years younger. He explains that while millions exert energy in the form of strenuous exercise in the search for health and self-improvement, it can only take them halfway on the quest.

"You are only what your inner mechanics allow you to be," he says. "With zone therapy, you can work every gland and organ in your body up to 100 per cent capacity. In the 1990s zone therapy will be the thinking persons' approach to health and beauty."

Of all the people who come to Joseph Corvo from all walks of life, there are not many whose ailments are not in some way stress-related. But without a doubt, the biggest single problem Corvo comes across is backache. "Just walking around on hard pavements can cause it," he says.

When a client visits Joseph Corvo for the first time they are invited to lie down and relax and talk about their problems and their lifestyle. Then, once he has a clue to their illnesses, he will take their feet in his hands and start to explore the organs of the body through their corresponding zones in the feet. "If you're sweeping out a room, you start at the extremities," he says. "In the same way, I start at the feet."

The Princess visits Corvo at his Bayswater flat where she sits on the edge of the bed in his small bed-sitting room and he tweaks her feet vigorously for half an hour.

Self-help is at the heart of Joseph Corvo's programme. With the help of his books and video, anyone can learn to massage the appropriate pressure points on the face, ears and neck, tongue, hands and feet.

If it is so easy to massage your vital organs yourself, surely there could be a danger of over-doing it? Joseph Corvo denies this. "No way can you hurt yourself. It's absolutely safe. It's natural and it works."

T'ai chi

The Princess of Wales has recently become a convert to t'ai chi, the ancient Chinese martial art which has become fashionable among high-powered city types, as a way of relaxing.

Charlie Chang, a hairdresser at Michaeljohn and a t'ai chi expert, says that it opens up the meridians of the body and calms the whole system. "After taking a class recently, my flu completely disappeared. After a session the whole body feels alive. It's becoming very trendy among people who are stressed out and who use it as an antidote to these modern times."

Difficult to master, t'ai chi takes a long time to learn and even longer to perfect. It consists essentially of a series of continuous, slow, smooth, graceful movements executed with suppleness and in a relaxed manner.

The moves are made with the body upright and completely straight with relaxation transferring the body weight to the legs. The more a person relaxes, the greater the weight that sinks down to the legs with a straight posture permitting the flow of energy.

The majority of t'ai chi exponents use it for exercise rather than as a martial art. It stimulates blood circulation, loosens and limbers up joints and at the same time promotes mental relaxation. It is very good for straightening the spine and improving posture, too.

It also exercises the cardio-pulmonary system. Just one half-hour workout is equivalent to the exercise derived from a three-hour game of golf, yet it is less intensive than either squash or tennis. Many of its new devotees like it for its convenience. Only ten minutes' exercise is required, it needs no special equipment and it can be practised in a small area.

Acupuncture

Another Oriental practice which the Princess uses is acupuncture, in which special very thin needles are inserted into the body at particular points in order to relieve pain and cure various disorders.

"I am very enthusiastic about acupuncture," the Princess has said. "It helps me to keep calm and relax." She has been having weekly sessions for about three years now and says she really enjoys it – it stops her from panicking and has enabled her to grow her once-bitten fingernails into elegant talons.

Massage

The Princess regularly has shiatsu massage, also known as Japanese finger pressure or acupressure, again to help her relax. This is a form of massage in which intensive pressure from the fingers and thumbs is slowly exerted over the whole body.

Health farms

One of the Princess of Wales' greatest treats was three days she spent at Champneys health farm in Hertfordshire in January 1990. It was an inspired Christmas present from Prince Charles, designed, not as a dietary regime, but as a relaxing, giggly respite from the world with her best friend Kate Menzies.

Booking in in the name of her lady-in-waiting, Anne Beckwith-Smith, the Princess enjoyed steam treatments, facials, saunas, swims and massages. She certainly didn't opt for the rigid lemon-and-water regime associated with health farms of the past. Instead, she enjoyed the companionship of the exercise classes and discovered the sybaritic pleasures of the whole spectrum of beauty treatments.

The only surprising thing about Diana's visit to Champneys is that she had taken so long to discover the benefits of a health farm. The appeal of a place like Champneys is that it offers so many of the things that she enjoys most – an ideal combination of exercise, healthy eating and luxurious beauty treatments, all under one roof.

The only essential element missing at a health farm is total privacy, and that may explain why, to date, Diana has only paid one visit to a place she so obviously enjoyed.

10
Back to
The Future

*P*rincess Diana has been a shining example to the
fashion world, and Britain's best possible fashion
ambassadress. One of her outfits can be headline news
right round the world. But with the coming of a united
Europe, will she widen her wardrobe and experiment with
wearing the top international labels?

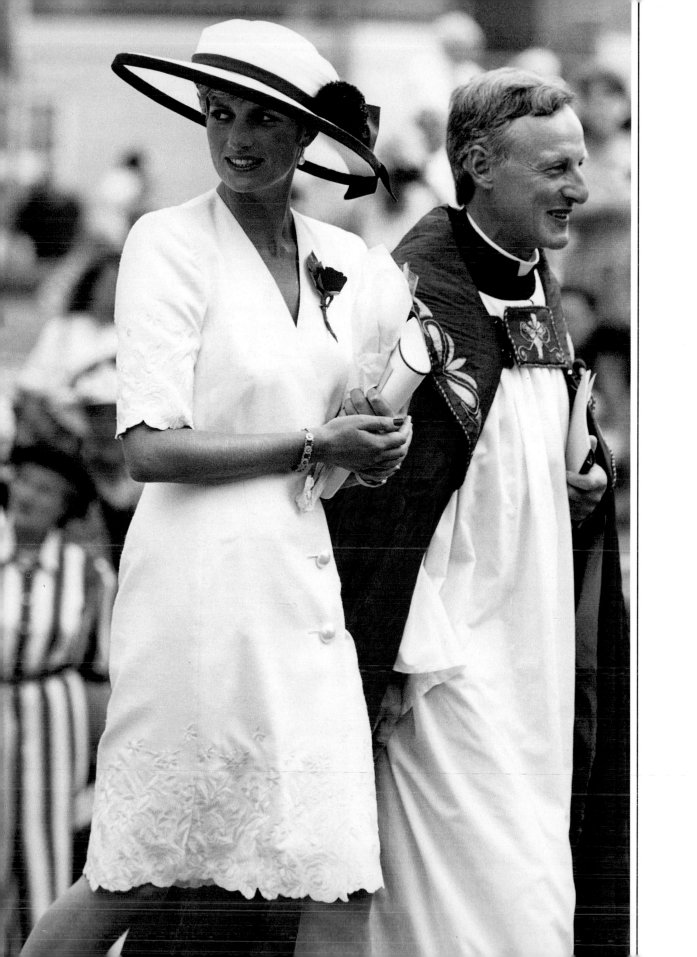

The Nineties is the decade of royalty. An era of recession is swinging away from the super-celebs of the Eighties and the super-models of the beginning of the Nineties and replacing them with the young royals.

The restoration of the European monarchies is no longer an impossible dream – and so the hitherto little-known princesses of France, Yugoslavia, Bulgaria, Italy and Greece are now raising their profiles.

Princess Helene of Yugoslavia models Paris couture from Lecoanet-Hemant in Paris and France's Princess Clotilde d'Orleans wears Dior, while the Princess of Wales is the favourite cover girl of British *Vogue*.

Ten years ago people were obsessed with fashion icons. Today it is the royals who offer us an escape from reality. It's also a safer view of fashion – beautiful, elusive but never vulgar nor over-indulgent.

Fashion seen on a model girl is unattainable, obscure and often ridiculous. Fashion, or beauty for that matter, viewed on a "real" person, even if they are royal, is delightfully tempting. The possibility that we could actually look as good as they do given the right hairdresser, make-up artist, fashion adviser or couturier, is undoubtedly exciting.

Not since the Fifties, when Grace Kelly married Prince Rainier of Monaco, and Rita Hayworth married the Aga Khan, has royalty seemed so glamorous. At a time of relative austerity it satisfies a craving for richness, splendour, and sheer escapism.

Shining examples

The young royals, are shining examples of the royal influence, and the metamorphosis of Princess Diana is a case in point. If the Princess has changed so dramatically in the last few years, just where will she be taking us over the next decade?

It may well be that, with the unification of Europe very much to the front of everyone's minds, the English royals will see this as the moment to dress more internationally – still flying the flag for British fashion, but at the same time picking from the cream of Parisian and Italian couture.

Princess Diana has done more for British fashion than any other single person; she is the best possible fashion ambassadress that Britain could possibly have. Every time she puts on a different pair of tights, the cash registers start ringing as millions of admiring women follow her lead. Each outfit she wears has an influence on the high street.

But these days, while her clothes still set as many trends as ever, she maintains a lower profile as regards their origin, preferring her charities rather than her designers to receive the publicity.

When in Rome...

And while in public Princess Diana prefers to follow the unwritten royal law of wearing British design, she has recently broken this rule for the sake of diplomacy. She chose a red Chanel suit designed by Karl Lagerfeld for a visit to Paris; a cream Escada coat for a tour of Germany; and a green Moschino suit for the London visit of the Italian president.

The young royals will play this new game of fashion diplomacy more and more, wearing Roman in Rome, Japanese in Japan, and captivating their captive audiences as never before.

In private, Diana wears Moschino, Kenzo, Chanel and Valentino. And her boldly checked red-and-black Moschino suit worn for Princess Eugenie's christening did manage to slip out of the country and appear on the royal tour of Canada.

Now that Diana has tasted the fruits of European fashion she may be tempted to buy

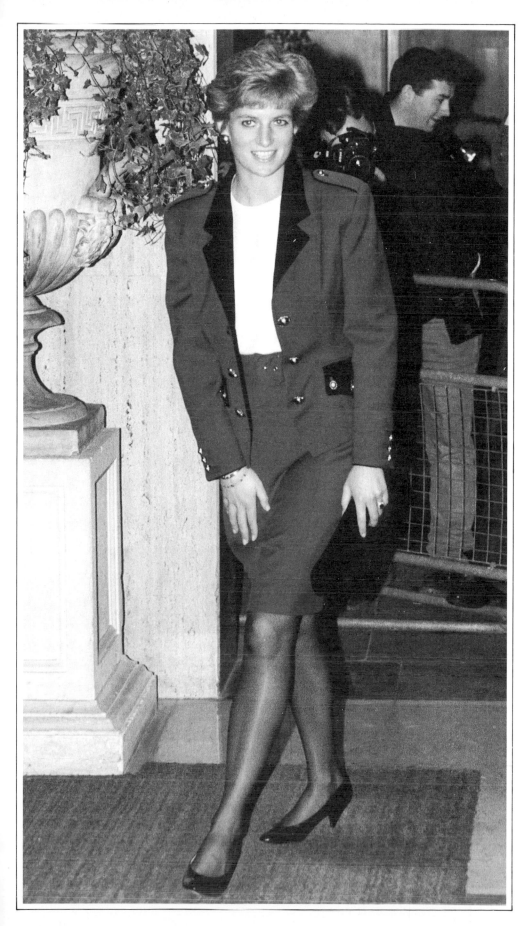

In public, Princess Diana generally follows the unwritten royal law of wearing outfits by British designers, but she has broken this rule several times lately for the sake of international diplomacy. This suit, by the Milanese designer Moschino, was chosen for the London arrival of the Italian President.

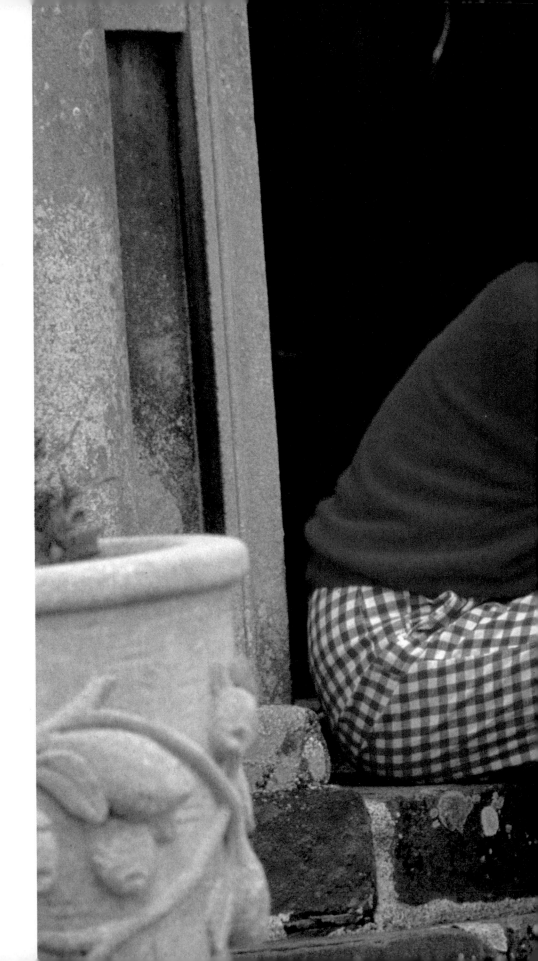

With the approach of the twenty-first century, royalty holds a greater fascination than ever, and no one more so than the Princess of Wales. Whether dressed in the most elegant of haute couture evening dresses or in casual separates, as here, she has a unique glamour.

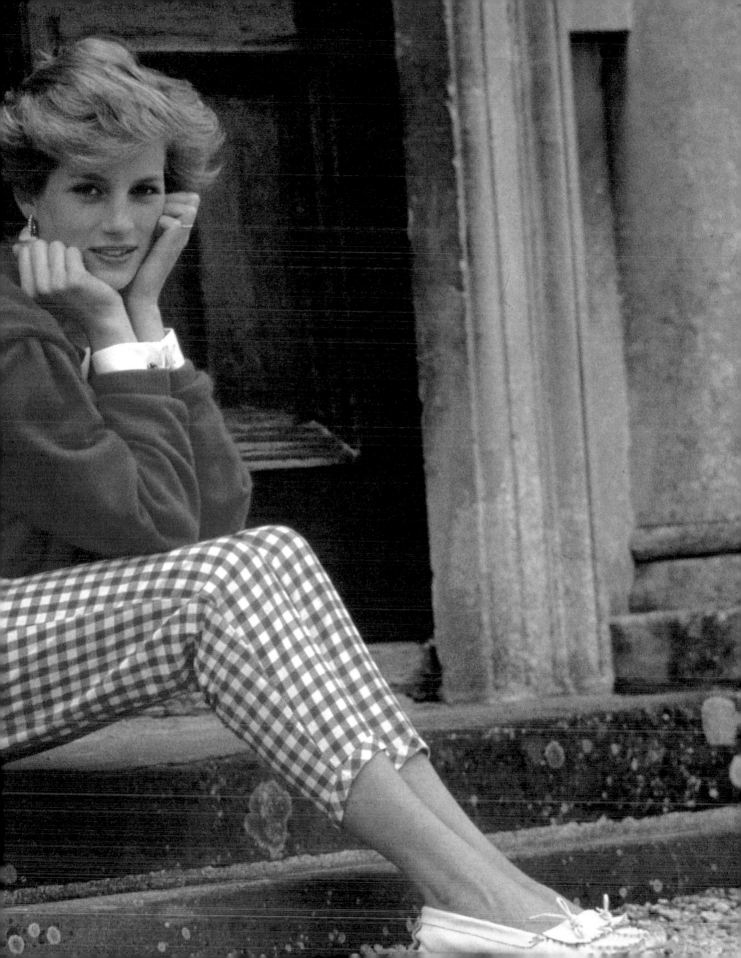

from Yves St Laurent. Not so many years ago, the Queen Mother, the then Princess Elizabeth and Princess Margaret all dressed discreetly but frequently in Paris couture. They dressed at the House of Lanvin in the Rue de Faubourg St Honoré, at Nina Ricci, at Christian Dior in the Avenue Montaigne and at a private dressmaking business in the Rue Royale next to Maxim's.

In a newly unified Europe, with the major designers using Paris as a communal fashion base whether they hail from Paris, London, Milan or Madrid, dressing European will almost certainly be the chic thing for the future Queen of England to do.

The allure of couture

The Princess of Wales, as she grows older, will no doubt increasingly value the quality and luxury of couture clothes. Dressing off-the-peg is all very well for a twenty-year-old size ten. But, as the Princess approaches her forties, she will appreciate the flattery of clothes which have been made to measure, after several fittings; which are in impeccable fabric and are lined with silk; and which are exclusive to her and her alone.

As a woman constantly in the public eye, not for her the unlined skirt that crinkles and creases. Not for her, either, the mass-produced print that can be seen in any high street, or the ill-fused interlining that spoils the line of her jacket.

The Princess can no longer afford to bump into Mrs Europe wearing the same outfit. She has the money, the resources and the taste, so it is extremely likely that she will increasingly buy haute couture, be it from London, Paris, Rome or New York.

London designers

Princess Diana has by no means ignored the tiny band of London couturiers. Victor Edelstein and Catherine Walker may be her favourites but she has also ventured into the rather stately Savile Row salon of Hardy Amies, a favourite of the Queen who is also patronized by the Duchess of Kent and Princess Michael.

Princess Diana's latest choice, the young Polish designer Tomasz Starzewski, who designs fun couture for the smart set, is actually the first couturier to open a London salon in forty years.

When Marc Bohan (who had previously designed for the grand Paris house of Christian Dior and dressed both Princess Caroline and Princess Grace) was hired by the hallowed House of Hartnell, favourite of both the Queen and the Queen Mother, he had high hopes of dressing the young royals. In fact, the Princess seems to regard Hartnell as still very much the Queen's territory and has so far not ventured to buy. She has made it her business to find out all about the new excitement at Hartnell and see the videos; but she prefers, in the main, to use couturiers who are particular to her and not to the rest of the royal family.

Supporting young talent

Given the opportunity (and approval from the Palace) Diana will dress more frequently at Moschino, flying discreetly to Milan or visiting him at his soon-to-be-opened London base. Once asked who he would like to model his outfit for a charity fashion show, the zany designer asked for the Princess. It's the sort of thing she just might do one day – she did, after

Fashion illustrator Nino Caprioglio predicts how Princess Diana might look dressed by Karl Lagerfeld in his svelte new longer-length leather look for Chanel.

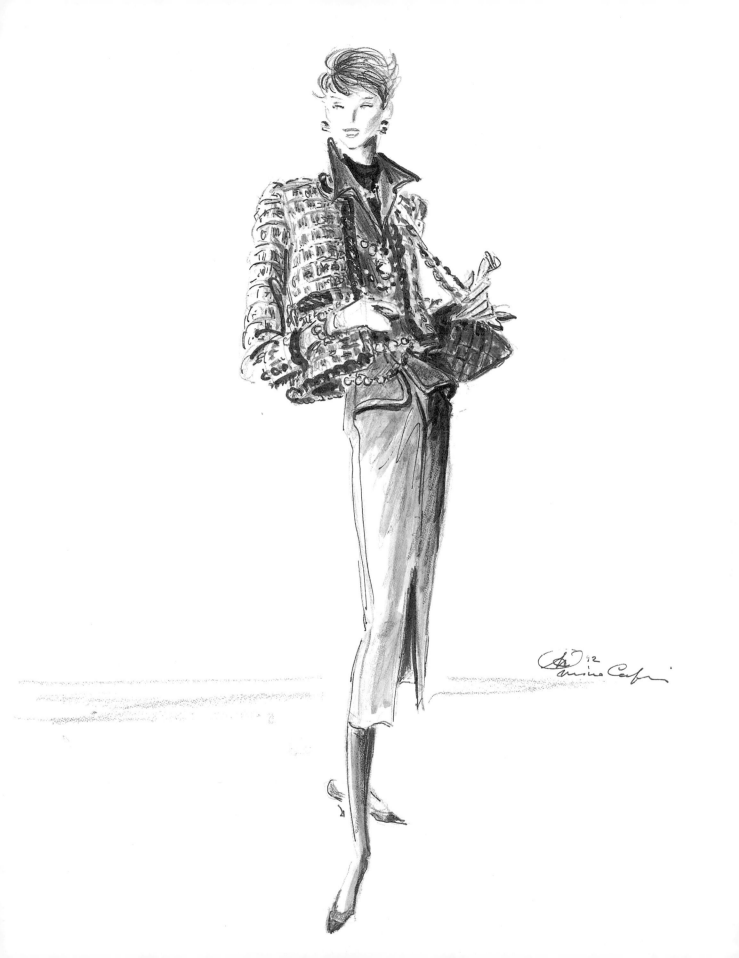

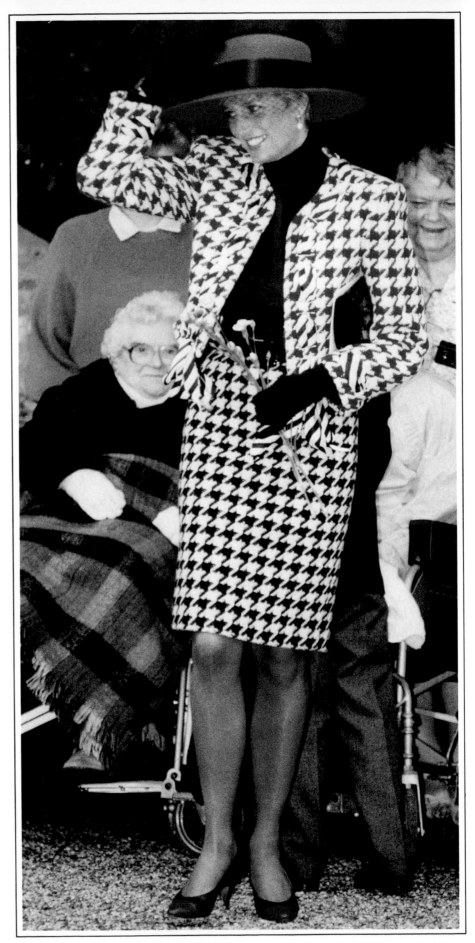

While Princess Diana likes to keep her penchant for international fashion strictly private, it is beginning to overspill into her public life now. This favourite Moschino suit, originally worn for the christening of Princess Eugenie, has appeared more than once in public. The juxtaposition of red-and-white jacket with black-and-white skirt was the Princess's own idea.

all, take to the stage of the Royal Opera House to dance with Wayne Sleep!

Diana has already expressed enthusiasm for the designs of Paris's youngest couturier, the immensely talented and creative Christian Lacroix. She once told him that she had watched the video of every one of his shows. He in turn is a great admirer of the royal family. He once designed a collection around the Queen Mother and her compatriot, the late Lady Diana Cooper.

Alexandre ... or Oribe?

And while she's at his chic salon in the Faubourg St Honoré, what would be more convenient than popping around the corner to visit the famous Alexandre de Paris to get her hair done. The elderly *coiffeur* is still the best in Paris, creating hairstyles for all the top designers. He is an expert with tiaras – the late Princess Grace was an Alexandre client as is her daughter Princess Caroline. (It was while she was having her hair done at Alexandre's that Princess Caroline learned of the death of her second husband.) Diana will have heard all about Alexandre from her ex-hairdresser Richard Dalton, who looks on him as a mentor.

On her visits to New York, the Princess might find it convenient to get her hair done by Oribe, the Big Apple's hottest hairdresser, who is now ensconced in the luxurious Elizabeth Arden Red Door Salon on Fifth Avenue – seven whole floors of fashion and beauty with wonderfully pampering beauty treatments.

Certainly, Oribe would love to get his skilful scissors onto Diana's tresses. He is a great personal friend and admirer of Diana's own hairdresser, Sam McKnight, but Oribe personally feels that the Princess should grow her hair.

"The English will hate me for this," he says, "but I think with longer, looser hair she could do more with it and it would be younger and sexier. It would be great longer for both tiaras or pony-tails and much more versatile."

While the royals muster the best advice possible from their designers, couturiers, hairdressers and make-up artists, there are many others out there ready to offer new advice.

Possible new directions

Although Princess Diana tends to cultivate her own favourite couturiers and keep them to themself, she has also worn a variety of others, including Bellville Sassoon, Edina Ronay, Alistair Blair, Chanel and Moschino.

Why shouldn't she experiment a little more in the future? Diana with her slim, model-girl figure would look marvellous, for example, in one of Saint Laurent's sophisticated smoking outfits. And she would no doubt appreciate the tailoring of Jean Paul Gaultier with its zany, avant-garde approach. She would also enjoy the stylish elegance of Karl Lagerfeld's own salon – she already buys his designs for Chanel.

Lower-profile young royals

As they mature we are likely to hear more too of the other young royals – the serenely blonde and beautiful Lady Helen Windsor, the vivacious Lady Sarah Armstrong-Jones and the avant-garde Marina Mowatt. With no royal duties to perform, they do not have a State allowance – let alone a budget for clothes.

Lady Sarah Armstrong-Jones, daughter of the Queen's sister Princess Margaret and fashion photographer Anthony Armstrong-Jones (Lord Snowdon), has a neat solution to her fashion problems. During her lunch-break from her job at an art gallery she pops in to see her friend Jasper Conran in Great Marlborough Street just off London's Regent Street. He advises her on her latest outfit before they go round the corner for a quick lunch. Jasper must have been delighted when Lady Sarah made it onto the 1991 International Best-Dressed List.

Lady Sarah keeps a low profile when it comes to clothes. She cycles to work and does not need special outfits very often. The exceptions are grand family occasions like weddings and birthday parties. She gets her hair done at Michaeljohn, where so many of the royals go. The salon is expert at twisting long hair which, like Sarah's, is usually worn casually, into grand knots topped with tiaras.

Lady Helen Windsor, who is engaged to marry art gallery owner Tim Taylor, is one of the prettiest of the young royals. The daughter of the Duke and Duchess of Kent, she has no royal duties or State allowance, and therefore has neither the need nor the budget to spend on fashion and figure. She will occasionally go to Victor Edelstein for a special ballgown, but usually her clothes are the normal girl-about-town's special mix of separate pieces gathered over the years and put together cleverly in different ways.

Lady Helen has not only a fabulously curvy shape, but also long honey-blonde hair and a skin that goes gloriously gold in the sun, rather than burning before browning as Diana's skin does.

Another young royal who cares little for haute couture is Marina Mowatt, daughter of Princess Alexandra and Angus Ogilvy. Married to photographer Paul Mowatt, Marina has become known for her avant-garde outfits which are fashionable among the club set she moves in but very different from her Buckingham Palace background.

International vote of approval

Best-dressed or less-dressed – what is the international vote on the royal family? The International Best-Dressed List is put together each year by an independent panel who judge a questionnaire which is sent out to every fashion professional worldwide – not just people in the fashion industry, but also people who watch fashion such as chic restaurateurs.

It is headed by Eleanor Lambert, who, in her late eighties, is still the doyenne of American fashion. She is a great royalist and believes in living the life of the rich and famous, whose style she documents. Frequently a guest at dinner parties attended by members of the royal family, she launched Marc Bohan's collection for the royal house of Hartnell.

The ultimate accolade

Princess Diana first joined the ranks of the Best-Dressed in 1981 along with the actress Jacqueline Bisset and Paloma Picasso. She was still there the next year, joined by Prince Andrew, who was voted one of the Best-Dressed Men along with the actor Jeremy Irons.

By 1983, Diana had received the Best-Dressed Citation for "the world's most influential woman of fashion today … not only the year's overwhelming favorite for her personal elegance but the inspiration for a sweeping trend away from eccentricity and toward dressing up". By 1984 she was cited as "Perennial Role Model of Fashion" and in 1985 Princess Diana and President and Mrs Reagan were cited as "today's three greatest influences in the world on the way people dress". By 1989, the Princess was safely ensconced in the List's Hall of Fame.

Although the Princess has long admired the work of the Parisian designer Christian Lacroix, she has not, as yet, worn his clothes. His lively mixes of colour and pattern – as shown in this strapless ballgown of silk taffeta – could give her wardrobe a whole new dimension.

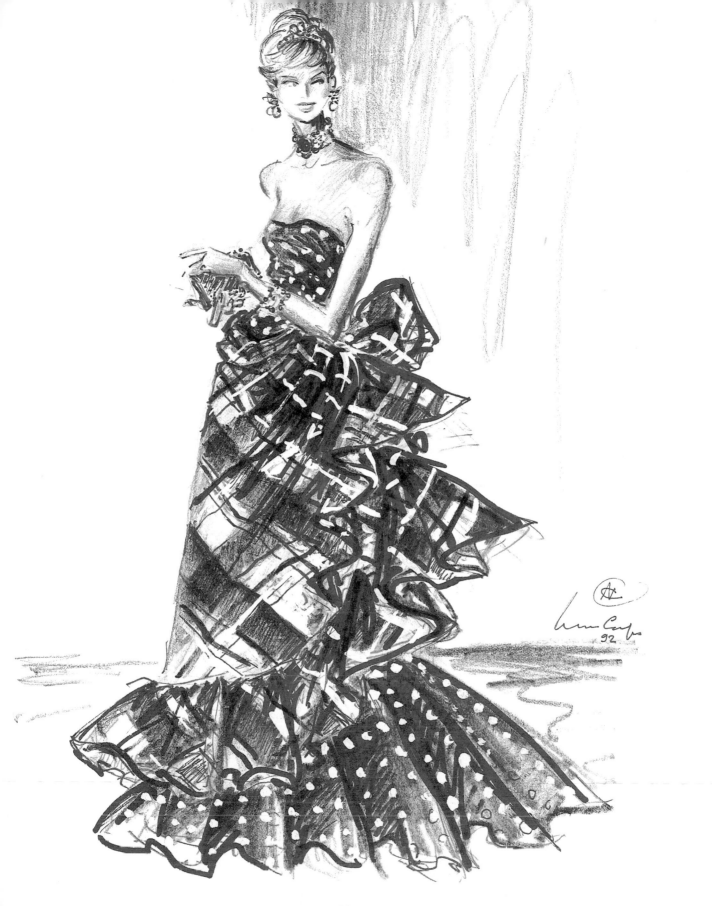

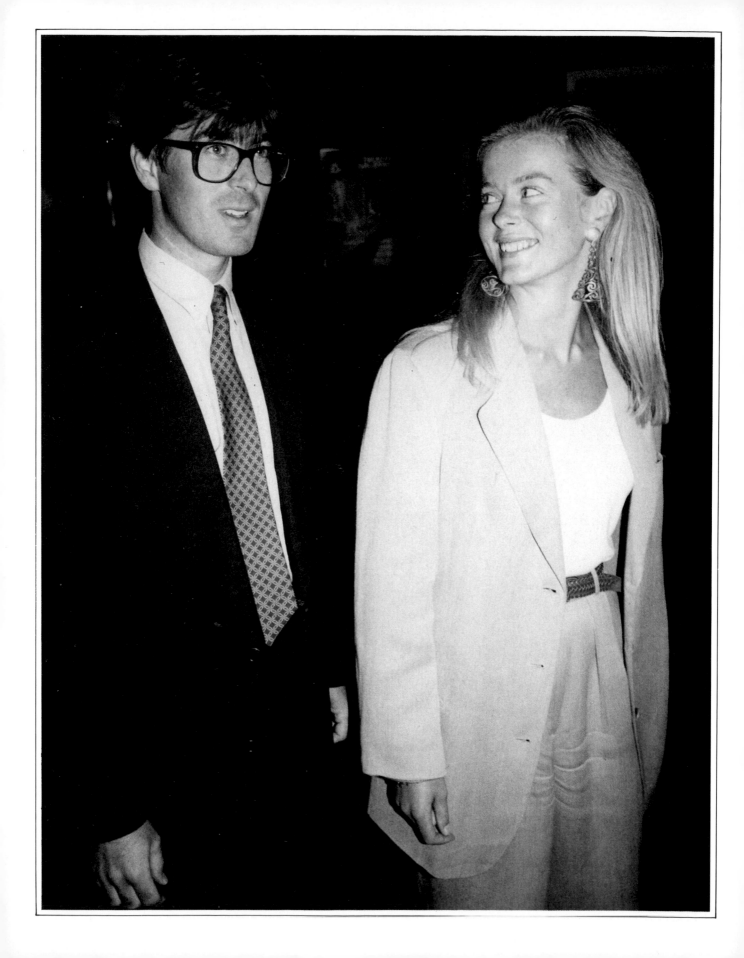

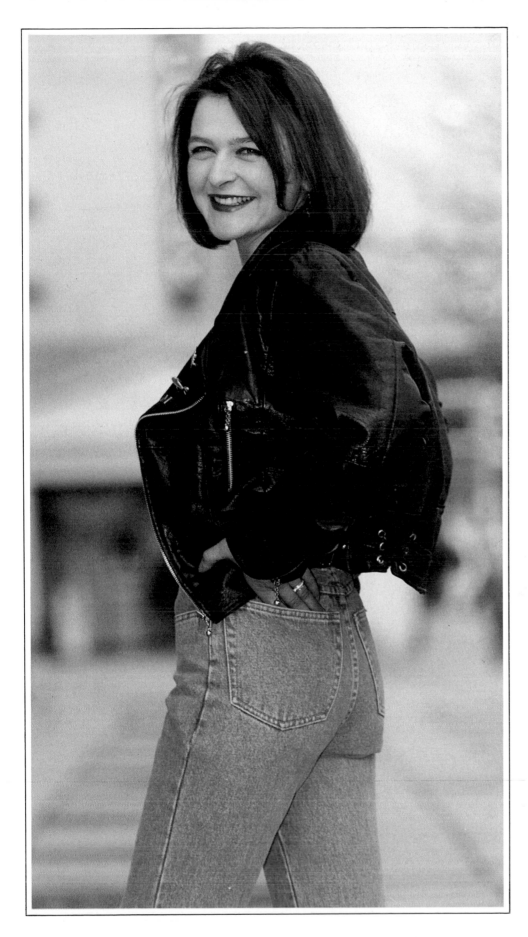

With the increasing interest in royalty in the 1990s, attention is focused on a number of the other young royals. Lady Helen Windsor (far left) has a stylish simplicity when it comes to fashion. A strong believer in the less-is-more approach, she loves the pared-down designs of the Italian fashion maestro Giorgio Armani – a taste that is shared by her mother, the Duchess of Kent. Marina Mowatt, née Ogilvy (left), the daughter of Princess Alexandra, has a decidedly unroyal fashion style, making headlines with her penchant for the rubber and leather fashions currently enjoyed in the underground club scene.

Index

Figures in italics indicate captions to illustrations.

Acknowledgements

The author and publishers are grateful to the following for
permission to reproduce photographs:
Tim Graham : pages 19, 20, 25, 55, 57, 58, 75, 83, and 114/115
Rex Features : pages 56, 61, 69, 73, 76, 80, 86, and 97
All other photographs : Express Newspapers